First published by AuthorHouse 01/25/05

ISBN: 1-4184-8071-1 (e)
ISBN: 1-4184-8072-X (sc)

Printed in the United States of America
Bloomington, Indiana

This book is printed on acid-free paper.

Table of Contents

To Pat
My friend,
my love, my wife;
the model of
beauty and purity
in my life

Foreword

"The Clear Path Home" reflects Jim's passion for souls. Nothing excites Jim more than seeing people come to faith in Christ and growing in Him.

No matter where you're at, no matter what you've done, it's possible to find *The Clear Path Home* and become the person that God destined you to be. *The Clear Path Home* articulates the simple truths underlying the realization that God passionately desires to have a relationship with each of us. Jim's book is a roadmap for your steps onto *The Clear Path Home*.

Dave Engbrecht
Senior Pastor
Nappanee Missionary Church
Nappanee, Indiana

Chapter One
Spiritual Personalities

*Then Agrippa said to Paul, "Almost thou
persuadest me to be a Christian."*
Acts 26:28 King James Version

*Then Agrippa said to Paul, "You think it a small task
to make a Christian of me [just offhand to induce me
with little ado and persuasion, at very short notice]."*
Acts 26:28 The Amplified Bible

This Son of a Worm-Eaten Wonder

Worms ate his father. They munched him away to a deplorable death, entirely lacking in glamour. Before that, his father went bankrupt, but then he managed to fight his way back, becoming a powerful and fearful king. On the last coherent day of his life, his father sat enthroned before the people of the cities of Tyre and Sidon, wearing a robe woven with silver thread. They were attempting to placate their king and smooth over an old feud, because their cities depended upon his benevolence for their food. In response, the king decided to deliver a speech.

As the sun slid above the horizon, the early morning beams reflected off his silver robe with an astonishing otherworldly brilliance. Addressed by this glowing, glowering monarch, the people were awestricken, if not also hungry and politically astute.

"It is the voice of a god, and not a man!" they cried. Herod Agrippa I, king of Palestine, grandson of Herod the Great, received their adoration, and then immediately collapsed in unbearable pain. He was being eaten alive, they soon discovered, from the inside out by worms. Five days later he was dead.[i]

The son became king, albeit only a vassal king under Rome. He lived and slept with his sister, Bernice, his conniving, incestuous lover. Together they were visiting the Roman governor Festus, to pay him homage and proclaim their allegiance. With great pomp and ceremony King Herod Agrippa II, young and fit and handsome at thirty-one, and his equally impressive sister-wife Bernice entered the auditorium with the governor to hear from an infamous Christian radical.

Agrippa II was the last of the Herods, the final heir of a royal-political dynasty with a record for terror and violent opposition to the early Christian community. A recognized expert on the Jewish religious traditions and writings from which all of this Messiah business had spawned, he knew very well the Jews' habit for incessant controversy. Agrippa II held the power to appoint the Jewish priests and was the overseer of their Temple activities. And now here he sat, listening to a defense of the Christian faith by its most aggressive proponent, Saul of Tarsus.

What Chains?

The Christians referred to him as the Apostle Paul. The Jews accused him of a number of offenses, all stemming from his allegiance to the crucified Christ. As he happened to be a Roman citizen by birth Paul held certain undeniable rights, making the legal process delicate. Paul appealed to Caesar, although Agrippa suspected that he had done it only to get a hearing in front of the emperor, and everyone else along the way. It was a wily strategy, which Agrippa frankly admired.

Paul was smaller in stature than Agrippa had imagined. His reputation preceded him, and except for his height, both his person and his personality upheld it. He was quick-witted, wiry, worldly-wise, eyes blazing with determination and an unnerving depth of passion.

Agrippa chuckled aloud as Paul paced and gestured and pleaded, all the while dragging his prison chains after him. Rather than binding him, those chains became an odd sort of adornment, taking on a regal nature, trailing around wherever he led them and never in the least confining him. They were a testimony to the aura of freedom emanating from the man. Paul's guards seemed bewildered, but more, it was clear they viewed their captive with respect, perhaps even a sense of wonder.

To Hear or Not to Hear?

Paul made a strong case for The Way, as he called his Christian faith. Who would have guessed that a Herod would one day consider, with something akin to sincerity, the claims of this sect? Had not his great-grandfather, Herod the Great, become notorious for slaughtering the infants of Bethlehem when the Jesus about whom Paul preached was born?

Great-grandfather saw this "Messiah" as a political threat, and unsuccessfully attempted to eliminate Jesus shortly after receiving word of his birth. Agrippa's great-uncle, Herod Antipas, beheaded the forerunning prophet of Jesus, John the Baptist, and ridiculed and mocked Jesus just before Pilate crucified the "King of the Jews." And his father, Agrippa I, killed the Apostle James, and imprisoned the one who was known as the Apostle Peter, the recognized leader of the sect. Of course, not long after that he became worm fodder.

Uncomfortable, King Herod Agrippa II shifted in his seat next to Festus, the new governor of Judea. He wondered if what happened to his father that day long ago may have influenced his own thinking on religious matters and made him softer. This man almost made sense! At the same time something troubling, compelling and spiritual beneath the surface of his consciousness tugged at Agrippa's heart, forcing him to weigh Paul's words carefully.

The Christians claimed that his father was smitten with the worms by God Himself, because he accepted the worship of the people and failed to deflect their glory and yield it to God. Others asserted that he was eaten because of his grievous persecution of the Christian church, and still others attributed it to nothing more than careless dietary habits.

Now here was Paul, the exact opposite of Agrippa II's father, having every opportunity to use his impressive learning and his oratorical skills to vindicate himself and curry favor. Instead, he spent this famous moment on nothing but God-talk. Paul, too, was once a persecutor of the Christians. Not only had he become a Christian himself, planting churches all over the world, but he also served as Christianity's most strategic political advocate. Agrippa was amused and challenged that Paul, having an opportunity to defend himself, instead seemed intent only on advertising his God. His father could have taken a lesson.

Paul spoke of an encounter with Jesus when he traveled to Damascus, and how he was struck down and then heard the voice of Jesus. He spoke of the call that the Christ had imposed upon his life to preach the gospel to the Gentiles. He spoke of how the Christ suffered and died at the hands of the Jews and the Romans, and then purportedly was raised from the dead.

Paul said there was a universal human need for - how else could he say it? - a sort of "relationship" with Jesus, apparently initiated by one's belief in the sufficiency of his life, death and resurrection as the means of their salvation. Agrippa couldn't help seeing how this fit with the Messianic prophecies of the ancient Jews. Paul proclaimed the need for repentance from sin, followed by a turning away from the old way of life, proving one's sincerity by their good deeds. He seemed so cocksure, so rooted. It was obvious this had gone beyond mere belief and was now elevated to the level of indisputable fact for Paul.

Agrippa's Dodge

About this time Festus, ignorant of the prophetic basis for Paul's claims, interrupted, shouting loudly, "Paul, you're out of your mind. Your great learning has made you insane!" Agrippa wasn't so sure.

"Most excellent Festus," Paul replied respectfully, "I'm sane. What I'm telling you is true. It's solid and rational." Paul's eyes shifted to Agrippa.

"The king is familiar with all of these things. I know I can speak freely with him. Certainly nothing I am telling you has escaped his notice. After all, none of this was done in a corner!"

Paul held Agrippa's gaze. "King Agrippa, do you believe the prophets? I know you do."

Caught! This Paul was a wise character. He had been a prominent Jew. He had been what they called a Pharisee, a highly educated and deeply dedicated scholar and practitioner of the Jewish faith. He knew that Agrippa was thoroughly acquainted with the Jewish prophecies regarding the coming of the Messiah, and that he flirted around the edge of acceptance.

Agrippa knew of the prophet Daniel's timetable, and he knew that it might not have been a coincidence when Jesus made a grand entry into Jerusalem at the time of the Jewish Passover feast. The timing was exact, according to the prophecies. Perhaps it was more than a symbolic act on Jesus' part. He knew of Isaiah's depiction of a Suffering Servant who would bear the penalty for all of man's sin in order to provide a way of salvation. The prophecies *could* have been fulfilled in Jesus.

But Agrippa was a clever one, too. He would lose everything if he showed weakness at this point. While Paul pressed him for a decision, and as every eye in the auditorium turned toward him, Agrippa countered. It may even have been against his deepest instinct, but he would not allow this lapsed Pharisee, however convincing, to trip him into a public profession of Christianity.

"Oh! Almost thou persuadest me!" Laughter rippled through the room. "Do you think you're making a Christian out of me, Paul? Surely you can't imagine that it can be done with such little ado and in so short a time as this?"

Paul never wavered. "Whether it takes a little time or much, I would to God that not only you, but also all that hear me this day, were both "almost" and altogether as I am." A twinkle lit the apostle's eye. "Except," he added "for these chains."[2] More laughter, as even Festus joined in.

Agrippa's reply soon became the subject of boundless discussion. Had he been in earnest, or merely sarcastic? Was he open or closed on this issue? Some said he attempted to conceal genuine emotion and that he truly was caught on the edge of persuasion.

Others said he fancied himself to be a man of intellectual depth and was offended to think that Paul might consider him a potential convert to Christianity so quickly and with an argument so unsubstantial.

Some thought his answer was a taunt, while others interpreted it as a firm rejection.

Without having been there, without the advantage of reading Agrippa's face and hearing his tone, it was impossible to draw a firm conclusion. And there Agrippa wobbles still today, perched and teetering on the uncomfortable cusp of his uncertain convictions regarding Jesus Christ; Agrippa, stuck in the realm of the almost persuaded.

Henry and the Jet

On an average day, on an average commuter flight, winging it from Portland, Maine to Boston, Massachusetts, Henry Dempsey was in the pilot's seat when he heard a strange racket. With his copilot taking over the stick, Henry moved aft to investigate. As the jet flew above the Atlantic Ocean it jostled through a random air pocket and Henry lost balance, shouldering his way into the rear door, which had been clunking because it was improperly latched. With Henry's weight against it, the door popped open and Henry disappeared, sucked out into oblivion.

The copilot was aghast and sickened as the red indicator light flashed against the control panel, signaling the open door. As he requested an emergency landing at the next airport, he also disclosed the fate of pilot Henry Dempsey and asked for an immediate search to be made for the remains.

They discovered Henry's body shortly thereafter, but not in the ocean as expected. Henry was found clinging to the jet's exterior ladder and was very much alive. He had somehow managed to clutch the ladder on his way out of the plane, embracing it for a full ten minutes at 200 miles-per-hour, 4,000 feet in the air. As the craft screamed down onto the runway, Henry's head rode twelve scant inches above the rushing pavement. Legend has it that several minutes passed as they worked to pry Henry's fingers away from the ladder that day.[3]

Jets are a mighty fine means of conveyance, but not by Henry's method. He was neither on nor off that plane, although he certainly was committed to the journey. Clinging to the shell is no way to travel. Just ask Henry Dempsey. In my mind that's where I have Henry. Clinging to the shell of a fast-flying jet, not in, but also dearly hoping he wouldn't fall off.

Eutychus Falls Out of Church

The young man's purpose was understandable. The room was crowded, the air still and hot. The best hope of a breeze was at the large window, and the closer he could get, the more refreshing it would be, so he crawled up in the casing. There was a pleasant view of the courtyard from his third story vantage point. With no glass in this window, he could pull his feet up and sit sideways in the opening. It was the best seat in the house.

He had come to church. The Christians were meeting that Sunday to observe the Lord's Supper, and would hear from an important visiting leader.

9

The meeting was longer than usual, since the special speaker was planning to leave the next day. This was a young church, needing much instruction. The air was becoming oppressively thick, and occasionally the young man would catch himself nodding off.

As midnight came and went his defenses were completely overwhelmed and he slipped into a deep slumber. Then he fell, catapulting headlong into the courtyard below. When the people reached him, they found him dead. Most fortunately for Eutychus, the Apostle Paul was the guest speaker. Running down to the courtyard, Paul threw his own body on top of Eutychus, and by the miraculous work of God, "they took him home alive."[4]

Eutychus was truly "happy, lucky and blessed" that day, fulfilling the meaning of his unique Greek name. But whenever he crosses my mind I have him carelessly falling out of church that night, sleepy and bored, cracking his head on the courtyard cobblestones, apparently having found nothing whatsoever to keep him inside.

Chapter Two
Who is the Spiritual You?

What's Your Type?

I recently took a Ministry Insights evaluation. It identifies your personality type, and also assesses the degree to which you step outside of your core personality in order to better interact as a part of your professional team. For those of us who are "Lion-Beavers" according to this assessment, it just serves to encourage us in our already aggressive behavior. We see our shortcomings as strengths and we feel a sense of affirmation rather than consternation when we read that other, perhaps gentler types generally think we're heavy-handed, abrupt and egotistical. For the most part I end up saying, "Hurray for the Lions!" We're making our point and achieving our objectives, and there's certainly no need to change that.

At the same time, I really do have a bit of trouble with seeing this snapshot of my personality. In my heart of hearts there are imperfect elements of my personality coming through and I don't care to deal with them. I thought I was perfect, but this is telling me I might want to stop and consider, so I must find some time for introspection. Well, that's just one more thing heaped onto an overloaded schedule, as far as I'm concerned.

I somewhat resent this intrusion of reason into my comfortable preconceptions about myself. That may be the same effect you'll get out of the application I'm about to make, but let's blunder ahead with it anyway.

I see the individuals we've been discussing as some of the possible "types" of spiritual personalities. The necessary question then arises: *Which type is yours?*

The Festus Personality: Acutely Uninformed

In the first scenario we met Agrippa and Festus, along with the Apostle Paul. Festus actually welcomed the input of King Agrippa in this particular legal matter, since Festus had no real knowledge of the Jewish religion and certainly had no familiarity with Christianity. He felt unqualified as the mediator, so he leaned on Agrippa's understanding. I see Festus as a good representative of the "hard case" spiritual personality type. He knew little or nothing of spiritual matters, even though his constituency was largely motivated and governed by Judaism.

We discover a similar orientation toward, or actually *away from*, the understanding of things Christian in modern America. Although the large share of our history, our culture and our law is in fact based upon and profoundly influenced by Christianity, I fear the majority of our citizenry remains acutely uninformed as to its nature.

Festus was apparently happy to call in an interpreter. His uninformed mind drove him to conclude that Paul was a madman, rather than understand that Paul's argument for the Christian faith was based upon a long and accurate prophetic trail and the recent factual events of Jesus' life, death and resurrection as fulfillment of those prophecies.

With the Festus personality one is forced to wonder whether by closing his mind to the facts, or perhaps by choosing to remain ignorant of them, Festus had not also closed his heart to the faith. Festus already knew what he knew and that was enough for him. Or was it? Festus had been sucked into the vortex of acute spiritual ignorance.

The Agrippa Personality: Carefully Noncommittal

I also believe there are many Agrippa types floating along on the winds of indecision today. Agrippa is discerning but evasive, understanding but uncommitted. He is a political thinker and a worldly man. When he is confronted with what he well may recognize as the truth about Jesus as the Messiah I believe his response is a mixed bag of emotion, reason and careful, careful, careful self-positioning.

Agrippa won't allow himself to make a commitment that might define him in the public eye. He is concerned about what his constituency will think, not to mention his cronies and his family. His judgment might be questioned, his aspirations could be thwarted and his political persona assuredly will be blemished if he shows any spiritual weakness or leaning whatsoever at this point.

All Agrippa can see, never mind the facts, are the limitations and ramifications of following Christ, given the anti-Christian climate of his day. Christianity is too controversial and too unpopular for him to embrace. So Agrippa's spiritual personality becomes that of the artful dodger or the fence sitter. Does he truly need more "facts" as he considers the case for Christianity, or is he using that as a ploy or a sort of spiritual smokescreen?

Too, there is an aspect of submission that comes with any spiritual commitment one might make, and many of us see submission as a sign of weakness, as does Agrippa. It's a price he's unwilling to pay, either for the sake of appearances or for the damage it may seem to do to his ego. It appears that Agrippa has counted the cost of Christianity and considers it to be too high. Rather than potential profit, he sees only loss of influence, respect and power on Christ's side of the spiritual balance sheet.

Instead of an outright rejection, I think Agrippa feigns indecision, though the result is the same in either case. It isn't a question of needing more information, it's a question of his willingness to submit to the already apparent truth. Make no mistake: the way is clear but it is eclipsed by Agrippa's self-will and terrestrial pride. Agrippa has been sucked into the vortex of willful indecision.

The Henry Personality: Out of Control!

Now Henry is another case altogether. I know that Henry's predicament was not spiritual in nature, except I'm sure he was praying for his life as he never had prayed before. The reality of life and death could never have been closer for Henry than it was during that ordeal. In fact, I would be most interested in talking with Henry today, to see how his amazing jet ride affected his view of life. That part I don't know.

I see Henry's real-life experience as a symbolic illustration of another spiritual personality. When I think of Henry, I think of someone screaming through life with the barest of spiritual involvement. I see Henry being blasted by the elements, torn at by the winds of circumstance, change, competition, perhaps even tragedy, disaster and loss. He's clinging to the shell of a spiritual life, but not inside the vessel, so to speak. Perhaps he would like nothing more than to climb in where he would be protected and would be assured of a safe landing, but the whole whirlwind of life and the immediate pressures he is experiencing keep him from it. There is just too much going on at a velocity too great for Henry to pull it together, to pull inside.

Then, too, there's always the possibility that Henry doesn't even realize that an "inside" exists. Maybe he thinks this is all there is, whether for himself or anyone else when it comes to spirituality. Maybe he thinks he's bound to end up riding this shell to destruction and for him there isn't any hope for anything different.

It's my somewhat founded but mostly speculative opinion that another large segment of America, if not the world, could be found right alongside Henry, hanging like a draggled toy from the belly of a beast that is bigger, faster and much stronger than he, and that is, more than anything else, incomprehensible and capricious . . . heading wherever it wants to go. Do you ever feel as if you are on an uncontrollable rocket ride such as that when it comes to life in general? Will it ever slow down enough for you to get your spiritual bearings? Henry has been sucked into the vortex of life's overwhelming, dictatorial circumstances.

The Eutychus Personality: Apathetic Detachment

At last we have Eutychus. To me Eutychus characterizes spiritual apathy. He's lost his passion. He's lost the sense of newness and promise and the aura of the miraculous that his spirituality once held. Poor Eutychus! Caught sleeping in church. One classical biblical commentator, from an era when such behavior would have meant something, said of Eutychus, "But, though the thing [sleeping in church] is often done now, yet how seldom is a sleeper in a church furnished with an excuse for it. No practice is more shameful, disrespectful, and abominable, than that so common of sleeping in the house of God."[5] Yet, what can he do?

Spiritual lethargy has set in for Eutychus. The law of lethargy is like the law of gravity, with much the same effect. Perch a spiritually lethargic person on the ledge and he will invariably take a fall toward the courtyard of discontent or disengagement. His spiritual progress will lock up, forward movement will shriek to a halt and he'll go hurtling down.

I don't often get a cold or a sinus infection, but when I do and my head backs up it's as if I'm watching everything around me go on in slow motion, and my perspective makes me feel as if I have somehow become detached. I don't mind the discomfort so much except for the terrible loss of energy.

That's the way I perceive the Eutychus personality. Watching the spiritual parade pass by, knowing you should be in it, but unable any more to get up the energy for the effort. Perhaps you have even deluded yourself into believing that everything is OK with you spiritually, even though you have no spiritual passion and your relationship with God has brought precious little real change into your life. Then comes the inevitable drifting off and falling away. The Eutychus personality seems to me to be suspended in that languid fall. He may never hit the ground in a killing heap, but then again, he just might. Eutychus has been sucked into the vortex of damning spiritual detachment.

The Secret of Your Soul

When it comes to your spiritual personality, whatever you may find it to be today, we're talking about the disposition or attitude of your eternal soul, and souls are God's business, and souls are *serious* business. Souls with a bad attitude are lost, and God is deeply wounded when that happens. When souls are lost, God loses. His system loses. His grand plan for the ages loses. You may ask, "If God is truly the all-powerful, all-knowing, all-sufficient Creator, Sustainer and Sovereign of the universe how can he possibly lose in anything?" He loses because he has chosen to lose. He loses because he has chosen to love. Where there is no risk of losing there is no love, and God has, above all other things, chosen to love you.

For Souls

I often will sign a letter or a more formal email under the closing "For souls, . . ." I do that because I have come to understand that souls are, as Bill Hybels is fond of intimating, God's only wealth. Souls are the standard by which he measures the value of everything else. We used to have a gold standard backing our currency in America, so in that regard gold was our standard of wealth. People are God's standard of wealth. You are God's gold standard. God still owns the wealth of the universe, but your soul is more important to him than all of that. *Your soul . . . you . . .* are God's only wealth, a secret not many come to appreciate or accept in this world.

The souls of men and women and boys and girls have become precious to me because they are precious to the God I love and serve. I love souls because He loves souls, and I strive to "persuade" souls into His eternal kingdom because that is God the Father's stated purpose in this world through His Son Jesus Christ. *"For the Son of man is come to seek and to save that which was lost."*[6]

I am willing to contend for the eternal welfare of your soul, but as important as that may be to me, I am not nearly as heavily invested in your soul status as is God. I just want to come alongside the work of his Spirit in your life and join him, but the initiative is his. He is the Father who longs to be reunited with his estranged child. He is the Husband whose heart burns with fervency for his bride.

Whether you see yourself clearly in one of our spiritual personality types, or whether you're somewhere, anywhere, in between, God wants your soul. He's passionate about it and holding nothing back; he is out to win your soul. There's the secret! Don't forget it.

God has made a number of appeals to you, through reason, through creation, through the people who have become what he calls his Body, the Church, through circumstance and through his Word, among other means. God calls for you in the midst of the chaos that defines your life and your heart. I know he does that, because he has done it for me. And I know that he is calling for you now.

Chapter Three
Original Faith

Attractively Off-Balanced

We're no different, you and I. I'm not imagining that I'm so much better than you. We all cry out to God from the imbalanced off-center of our dizzy lives, not from the balanced center of our perfectly arrayed priorities. Festus, Agrippa, Henry, Eutychus, Jane, Mary or Percival, there is a place within each of us, perhaps only visited in the middle of the dark night, where we are desperate for God. That's good, because it is our desperation, not the perfect order of our lives, which drives us to seek God.

Desperation is an essential element of our spiritual "connectability" with God, and I'm quite sure that desperation and perfect order never coexist in this life. So if your spiritual personality profile indicates you have some disorder in your house, don't become discouraged and give up; instead, press on. There are so many of us who are frantic for a hint of God's presence, urgently straining to see through the deep blindness of spiritual obscurity, self-induced though it may be. Those are the personality types to which God is attracted, so God is attracted to you right now; you and your imbalance, I and mine.

Hanging by a Thread

I'm not kidding myself. We Christians don't have it all together. We're hanging by a thread. One thread. I'm speaking to you from this dangling place of my own, fixed to my thread. It's a scarlet thread, unbreakable, but a thread nonetheless. It is a thread of God's making; a thread of God's sustaining. And we're willing to share our thread. We're hanging by a thread, but Oh! What a thread! This thread I'm referring to is our Christian faith in what we mean to God, and what he has done, is doing and will do for us.

It is our Christian faith, admittedly as it is challenged by our fragile humanity, but also as protected and perpetuated, renewed and strengthened by God himself. This thread is our faith, which he has given us as a gift, for we never could have imagined such things for ourselves. It is our faith that remains firm despite our spiritual ADHD, as God enables us to zero in with supernatural focus upon his reality, his immediacy, and his faithfulness to us.

The Stuff of Faith

It's an amazing thing. God has made this provision and sustains this possibility from his Sovereign, loving prerogative alone. He has worked the works of Salvation entirely for us, on our behalf. But because of Love, indeed, by its very definition, he leaves the choosing to us. He has determined that our participation is required, while still having planted the seed of desire and the capability to embrace the mystery of eternal salvation deep within every human heart.

"Now to him who is able to do immeasurably more than all we ask or imagine, according to his

power that is at work within us, . . . "[7] God wants to do "immeasurably more" in your life, because you mean immeasurably more than all you might ask or imagine or hope to mean to him. I know this, I experience this acceptance and more, and I hope to add my tiny voice to his, to speak of that which I know in anticipation that you may be persuaded to join me as a child of God.

My prayer for you is that you will put whatever offbeat spiritual personality you have aside and consider God's passionate appeal to win your heart, and once considering, you will offer it to him, no strings attached and nothing held back. If you do, you will enter an extraordinary realm of life reserved only for those special ones God calls his sons and his daughters.

Chapter Four
Playing "Let's Assume"

Phooey on Convention! Let's Have More of the Mystery

I admit I bring a sense of urgency to this writing. I'm not interested in playing by the rules any more. I've tried that and it's ineffective at best and downright counterproductive at worst. I'm tired of rules that bind and rules that thwart, rules that confuse and rules that distort, but more importantly, I'm tired of words that diminish and words that divert, particularly when it comes to the discovery of eternal spiritual truth.

Once in a while when I'm online doing research I'll get ambushed by a nearly unending stream of popups, those annoying little advertisements that hijack your computer and misdirect your attention. They elbow their way gallingly into your path and mess up your agenda. They pervert the purpose of your research and steal your time. Some of them come from the site you're visiting, and others come from who knows where.

Life is like that, and spiritual life is especially so. There are many diversions that pop up in life regarding the essential, spiritually transformational truths of the Christian faith, and they originate both within and without the Church. God's work as it is accomplished through his Son Jesus Christ, carried out by the presence and the power of his Holy Spirit, is transcendent and transforming.

There is not enough transformation going on these days, and often it is our uncompromising pursuit of intellectual satisfaction that gets in the way of the Blessed Hope that emerges from the Blessed Mystery of Christ and the Christ-life. It is something that is described as a mystery containing glorious riches and defined as *"Christ in you, the hope of glory."* [8]

The Apostle Paul explained the process of relating and delving deeper into the mystery of Christ when he wrote, *"We proclaim him, admonishing and teaching everyone with all wisdom, so that we may present everyone perfect in Christ. To this end I labor, struggling with all his energy, which so powerfully works in me."*[9]

When our wisdom ends up resting upon the mystery of Christ, and when we labor to relate it to one another and to our world as we struggle *"with all his energy"* powerfully working within us, then I believe we have the right idea, and I believe we'll witness the result of God's intent. At times that means we step more into the mystery than into the understanding of it.

Let's Go There, But Just Not Now

The conventional approach by conventional rules to any conventional (and, therefore, normally harmless) spiritual investigation would insist that we must now first deal with all of the gaping holes in humanity's spiritual sense of reason. We're told we must do this before we can approach anything regarding our personal relationship with God. The rules insist that we make no assumptions whatsoever, laboriously arguing every issue to death and then resurrecting them all and thrashing them over again, particularly when the truth approaches mystery. The rules insist that we begin with God and attempt to determine whether or not he exists, and we must arrive at a scientific answer.

The simple fact is most of us already concede that God exists. We're more concerned with what, if anything, that should mean to us. Then in addition to that we must decide upon the matter of truth, and attempt to prove whether or not there is such a thing. Then we must move on to morality, then ethics, and by that time we will have forgotten what was the original point in all of this, which is to hear what God has to say to us and not so much what other people have to say about God.

Of course, that's either before or after we deal with our problems concerning Jesus. Is he a valid, historical figure? Did he do miracles? Was he truly crucified for the sins of the world? What about the resurrection? Was Jesus merely a great prophet or teacher, or was he truly the Son of God incarnate, God *with us*, God walking in our very midst?

We can discover the answers to these questions, however challenging they may seem, and more. We can settle these issues intellectually with abundant documentation and substantial proof. We can and we should, but I'm not sure that we *must* right now. The problem often takes this form: When we approach spiritual truth by conventional, rational means, we end up with a conventional, rational and entirely impotent and unsatisfying "product" that becomes the preferred object of our faith-life.

That generates a form of faith, which we then invest in the wrong thing, achieved by the wrong means, accomplishing nothing and leading nowhere. It is cerebral, but a purely cerebral faith, devoid of the spiritual stuff that feeds and fires the heart, can be very cold and empty, and our subtitle is, after all, *God's Passionate Appeal to Win Your Heart*. These intellectual pursuits have their time and place, but as a person susceptible to getting lost in the academic side of things I'm beginning to learn that God's appeal resonates with ideas much deeper and, carefully said, perhaps in some sense more important than our intellect.

We must find a middle ground somewhere, and that is our point with this argument. We must find the balance between the spirit and the intellect, appealing to both without stifling either. I find most of our experience in these things today tends to slide quite definitively to one side or the other.

Schaeffer's Pendulum

Francis Schaeffer was one of the most influential Christian philosophers of modern times. In his book *The Great Evangelical Disaster* he wrote,

". . . In this fallen world, things constantly swing like a pendulum, from being wrong in one extreme way to being wrong in another extreme. The devil never gives us the luxury of fighting on only one front, and this will always be the case."[10]

I'd rather forget the rules, instead starting with the main point, which is that your soul is hotly in play and God is making his bid for it. God loves you. He wants you as his child forever. You may not, however, sense that just yet.

A Lone Reed Calling to the Void

In the movie *You've Got Mail*, Meg Ryan's character is Kathleen Kelly, the owner of a children's bookstore. Kathleen is involved with Tom Hanks' character, Joe Fox, but at first only through an anonymous online relationship. They exchange a constant stream of emails, and begin falling in love. Kathleen is navigating a life crisis as her small book business suffers due to the opening of a book megastore nearby, which just happens to be owned by Joe's family. So she naturally begins pondering the "big deal" issues of life.

"I'm wondering about my work," Kathleen says to Frank, her current flesh-and-blood boyfriend. "I mean, what is it that I do? All I really do is run a children's bookstore."

"All that you really do," Frank earnestly responds, "is this incredibly noble thing. You are a lone reed! You are a lone reed, standing tall, waving boldly in the corrupt sands of commerce."

"I am a lone reed."

"Lone reed."

"I . . . am . . . a . . . lone . . . reed," Kathleen repeats pensively.

Later that night Kathleen sends a thoughtful message off to her inscrutable e-pal.

"Sometimes I wonder about my life. I lead a small life. Well, valuable but small. And sometimes I wonder, do I do it because I like it or because I haven't been brave? So much of what I see reminds me of something I read in a book when, shouldn't it be the other way around? I don't really want an answer; I just want to send this cosmic question out into the void. So, good night dear void."[11]

Many of us experience this life as if we're that "lone reed." In the dark of night we face the void within and from its unknown depths we cry to the void without. Void cries out to void. The very authentic void in the human heart is that juncture where our hardest and most bewildering questions, our sorest tender wounds, our truest sorrows, our unspoken fears and our grandest disillusionments are gathered together in one profoundly demanding, clamoring assembly. They must be attended. They must be met, they must be addressed, and they must be satisfied. (We'll discover later that God purposely constructed us that way. It's a built-in feature.)

Do you ever feel as if you're sending your questions and your vulnerabilities about the improbabilities of your life, your spirituality, and your significance out into a familiar but unresponsive void? Are you expecting an answer to come back? Do you even want one? Or is that void leaving you feeling cold, transient, loveless and skeptical, with nothing in which to believe? I guess what I'm really asking here is *how are the "voids" working for you in your life? Are they enough for you?* I doubt they are, if you're human.

What is There for Believing?

Most people come up short when it comes to believing in things, particularly when it comes to matters of the heart and soul rather than science. Janet Fitch writes an interesting scene in her best seller *White Oleander*.

"So what about love?" I asked.

"What about it?" . . .

"Don't you believe in it?"

"I don't believe in it the way people believe in God or the tooth fairy. It's more like the National Enquirer. A big headline and a very dull story."

"So what do you believe in?" I asked her.

"I believe in living as I like. I see a Stickley lamp, a cashmere sweater, and I know I can have it. I own two houses besides this. When the ashtrays are full in my car, I'll sell it."[12]

I propose that approach is not enough for any human heart to subsist upon. Thankfully, when we become caught between our everyday lives and our realization of the hulking void in our hearts, when we come up short on things in which we can unquestionably trust, God is there, and he can be believed. If we are to know him, however, we cannot, as unlikely as this may sound, allow reason, logic, rationality or disillusionment to get in the way. God is there, but these other things can, when improperly handled, veil his presence. He is fielding your wonderment, but more, he is speaking into the spiritual void in the center of your soul. He is not silent, but his voice is Spirit and it is up to you to listen, and then to respond, with your spirit.

God wants to fill the inevitable void and to establish a beachhead of the sacred in our lives. He is not detached. He wants to replace our emptiness with absolute fullness. He wants to burn away the suppressing enigmas and the killing boredom of our daily routines with the challenge of a meaningful eternity. He wants to bathe every moment of our existence in limitless significance.

But to make room for that amazing, passionate, divine possibility, and in order not to delay a moment longer, it's time to quit playing by the rules, because the rules of this life by which we normally play leave no room for God. The rules leave no room for the spiritual, no room for the transcendent. We go after the facts surrounding God and religion and we end up buried in them or running off on thorny rabbit trails. There is truth, there is reason, there is logic, and then there is transcendent Truth, transcendent Reason and the wondrously effective Illogic of the divine. These all belong to God, but he has willed them to us, daring us, desiring us, to become just irrational enough to seize our divine inheritance.

Come On, Let's Play!

That's why we must at this important intersection of spirituality, faith and reason leave off all of our seriousness and play a game. I call it "Let's Assume." Now, don't get upset at the idea of taking on some assumptions, and please hear me out on this whole thing. We must make assumptions every day and use things without first taking all the trouble of proving them.

Have A Seat

Forgive me the use of an old illustration, but we assume that a chair will hold our weight and therefore we sit. We don't first test it by piling on a couple of bags of cement to approximate our body weight. We don't even wiggle the thing or poke at it to assure that it has been properly constructed. We don't try the nuts and bolts of it or perform a chemical analysis or stress-test the glue.

We simply observe the chair, noting that it has been placed wherever it is with the obvious purpose of being employed for its intended use. We see that it appears to be intact, it appears to be of an appropriate design, and it looks reasonably sturdy. The chair has, by evidence of its wear, apparently proven to be a proper implement for sitting in the past, and so we sit. None of these assessments are even particularly conscious in most cases. They are instantaneous and unconscious.

Let's Play, but No Pretending

Notice I have called the game Let's Assume and not Let's Pretend. You see, that's the problem with most people's ideas about Christianity. They lump it onto the same heap as all the other systems of human thought calling themselves religion. Their basic thinking about religion is that it belongs in the same category as mythology or some sort of psyche-soothing pastime, or perhaps aromatherapy for the soul. They think, wrongly, that Christianity is about feel-good pretending. Chicken soup for the soul to be sure, but not a real prescription for dealing with the hardness of life, or a viable antidote for the problem of sin that's causing all of this hardness to begin with.

We're going to make better assumptions about Christianity than that. The assumptions we're going to make are much better than pretending because good assumptions are of a different substance. Good assumptions presume they are based upon fact, not fantasy, and thus have the expectation of proving valid and being fulfilled. Good assumptions serve to lead us into the realm of reality and discovery, not into the world of pastimes, entertainments, escapism or make-believe. True, poor assumptions may end up being disproved, but ours will not, because they're made of the proper stuff.

When it comes to playing Let's Assume regarding the Christian faith, we do so simply because we can. We're safe in doing it. This game will prove itself worthy, just as it has since Christ came. Even before he was physically born into this world the seed of Christianity, just the mere expectation of it, was worthy enough for men and women to stake their lives upon. After you've played our game, after you've finished this book, when you go back around to the beginning to pick up the puzzle pieces and fit them together, they'll all be there and they will match. They will work.

Don't Fall for It!

Now, as contrary as it may seem, I hope you'll allow me to argue as vigorously for making a properly informed decision for Christ as I have for embracing the mystery. Playing Let's Assume is the only way you can cross the threshold of mediocre living into the realm wherein hope, faith and belief give birth to a relationship with the Divine, and where everyday life and your longing for things eternal have the potential of merging. We must, however, enjoy perfect agreement on one important point: Playing Let's Assume is not just a way to get you to cut to the chase and jump into a personal commitment to Christ without thinking. It's a measured spiritual step, not the short-circuiting of the intellect.

If you are not satisfied to an acceptable degree intellectually, you are not ready for the spiritual venture that I am recommending. There are many devices that have been used to manipulate people toward the Christian kingdom, and I consider all of them undesirable while some of them are particularly low-grade. Let's take the idea, as just one of many possible examples, that God might turn his back on

33

you and cut you off from any hope of salvation if you don't decide right this moment to become a Christian, no matter what you think about it. Here's what I think God would say: *"Don't fall for it! It's manipulation!"*

I own a couple of Internet domains. I recently received an email regarding one of them from the service through which I maintain my domain ownership. The subject line read, "Your Internet domain requires attention." Naturally I opened the message, only to discover that there were some peripheral services they wanted to sell me. They got me to open up their pitch through manipulation. This was particularly stupid for a couple of reasons.

First, people don't like to be suckered. As a former professional salesman I can never understand anyone trying to sucker a customer. It only serves to harm the relationship and to irritate one's clients.

Second, there are all kinds of domain managers out there in cyberspace, and their competitors are continuously striving to get me to switch to their service. So if my current provider acts stupidly and incites me to go elsewhere for service, it's not a very long trip. None of this makes any sense in today's wildly driven world of information management.

Over-Promising Under-Deliverers

Another problem that keeps manifesting itself in the sales world is the tendency for sales professionals to over-promise and under-deliver. It doesn't take much imagination for either of us to immediately draw a comparison between an unprincipled used car salesman, an unscrupulous telemarketer, a scam artist and a televangelist. I occasionally listen to some of the late night televangelists, when I can tolerate the exposure.

Just a few nights ago I heard a story from an individual who represents himself as a teacher of God's deep wisdom for living. He is nothing but a fundraiser, primarily for himself but also for other "ministries." If I sound intolerant of these shenanigans, it's because I am and I'm not required to be gentle with behavior so far off kilter with God's intentions.

His story went like this: "I arrived at the airport in my limousine the other day. My elderly daddy was traveling with me. I sat back, watching in satisfaction as the limo bypassed the parking lots and pulled past the hangar and onto the tarmac that is reserved for the private jets.

"I was so grateful as my dear old daddy was able to skip all the security checks and the inconveniences that all the common people have to endure, and walked straight up the steps of my own personal luxury jet. And I thought, thankfully, how fortunate it was that years ago I made that first thousand dollar pledge, sowing a thousand dollar seed into the fertile ground of a real faith ministry - a powerful faith ministry, just like this one has become. And I thought, oh, if not for that seed, where would I be today? And where would my poor daddy be? He'd be slogging through the terminal with all the average people, that's where he'd be. I couldn't bear that thought.

"Now, I want to give you that same opportunity tonight. I want to extend to you the invitation, no, the privilege, of sowing a thousand dollar gift into this ministry, and God's going to bless you for it, my friend. He's going to multiply your gift miraculously, and you will reap the abundant rewards of your generous giving. Remember, he who sows little reaps little, but he who sows much shall reap in abundance!"

Call It What It Is

There is a great temptation here to rush down one of those rabbit trails I warned you about and spend a lot of effort in refuting this television garbage, but let's keep to the point. There is nothing true in that sort of drivel, other than the fact that the guy concocting it does indeed have his own private jet and a whole lot more, thanks to the hopeful but vain investments of thousands of gullible marks. His con works, that's for sure. But it only works for him. He over-promises and under-delivers and does it in the name of God. His reckoning will come.

The truth is, should you choose to respond to God's passionate appeal to win your heart, your life may not change all that much in the material realm. You might even meet bigger challenges and endure worse trials than you are presently experiencing, but you'll do it with the assurance of God's presence, with an eternal destiny guaranteed by his unbreakable promise. There is a transcendent realm in which God is inviting you to dwell.

Ignorant Misapplications

I think this all applies to the matter of faith. Perhaps a misinformed or erroneously inspired leap at the Christian faith is worse than your faith remaining inactive while you gather the essential facts and come to an understanding of the truth about God. Perhaps the missteps of well-intentioned but ignorant believers or unconscionable and ruthless televangelists in motivating you toward acceptance of the Christian faith could end up driving you toward the "competition." I hope to be more careful, and certainly more honest than that.

Some Christians, who do not have a good understanding about Christ and his passion, nor of their Bibles, try to use similarly defective tricks to rush people into believing. That's no good because it's trying to manipulate a decision out of someone on the basis of a faulty notion. If it's intended to influence people into the kingdom of God its result will be more like someone planting a new African violet in sand rather than the proper soil mix and then expecting marvelous purple blooms to burst out all over. Not gonna happen.

There is an overwhelming ignorance of Scripture, both within and without the circles of Christianity today. Sometimes Scripture is misused. Take another look at this back-turning business, as an example. It is based on the misinterpretation of Scripture, which does indeed tell us, *"Then the Lord said, 'My Spirit will not contend with man forever, . . .'"*[13] That is dealing, however, with the length of man's days on this earth

37

rather than the extent of God's offer of salvation and eternal adoption through Jesus Christ. Mechanisms of this type are a cheap way to get you to "Buy today! Act now, before this offer expires!"

That is not the way God works even though, as ever, God's Word stands true when he says, ". . . *In the time of my favor I heard you and in the day of salvation I helped you. I tell you, now is the time of God's favor, now is the day of salvation."* [14]

Now *is* the day of salvation, but truly, God isn't having a pre-fire, one-day-only, never-to-be-repeated sale on it. He expects you to bring your brains with you when you come to him. I have complete trust, as can you, in God's process for encouraging you to do so. That process belongs entirely to God and he doesn't need me to devise any marketing devices to help you along or to "close the sale." He has no "pot sweeteners" to entice you to jump into Christianity before you've gone through the appropriate process and weighed the costs. If anything, he cautions you against it! He has established a clear path leading directly to the heart of it, but he has also made it a path without any possible shortcuts. It is a package deal with specific requirements and no discounts. You deserve to know that up front.

Chapter Five
Faithbumps

Getting Ready for the Game: Faithbumps Ahead

In Chapter Three I proclaimed the reality of your faith by declaring that you have it, whether you recognize it or not. But simply because I proclaim your faith doesn't mean you must accept the fact of it or like it. So now comes an unavoidable speed bump, even before we get to the rules of the game. We must, somehow, come to an understanding about the substance and the application of such a thing as faith.

Whenever you play Let's Assume, it does indeed include a strong element of simple faith, and faith is often considered to be something less than intelligent and something less than dependable, concrete or advisable. Yet our assumptions are the primal genesis of a proper faith-life. Philip Yancey in his book *Rumors of Another World: What on Earth are we Missing?* says it well.

"'You need eyes to see and ears to hear,' Jesus said to those who doubted him. It takes the mystery of faith, always, to believe, for God has no apparent interest in compelling belief. (If he had, the resurrected Jesus would have appeared to Herod and Pilate [the government officials instrumental in sending him to his death by crucifixion], not to [those who were already his followers])."[15]

Faith is personal, concrete and experiential. It must be so for it to be any good at all. It doesn't exist

39

as some ethereal mist that is good only for pondering but nothing else, too vaporous to be grasped. It exists for a very real and very important purpose, but you must grab hold of it and try it on and then you must test it out as you might a suit of armor. If you're going to win the eternal spoils in this battle of your life, you need the armor. If you don't try it on, if you don't prove it, nothing of spiritual significance will ever happen in your lifetime, and you will have missed the whole point of having a life in the first place.

I read that there's a product called Bear Mace which comes with a warning: *Caution, may not work in all situations.*[16] I guess I'd like to know more about the situations in which my Bear Mace may not work before I wander off into the wilderness depending on it for protection. That's the same reason the knights of old would test their armor, and why you must test the whole concept of personal faith in God, so try it on! After all, you're being asked to depend upon it for your eternal well-being. There are a lot of promises being made about it, and if they're not true after you've chosen to follow the way of faith you could get hurt. So test it.

Understanding Basic Faith

In his book *Mere Christianity*, C. S. Lewis tells of an old R.A.F. officer who took exception to a reference Lewis had made to the study of theology in a talk he had just delivered.

"I've got no use for all that stuff. But, mind you, I'm a religious man too. I know there's a God. I've felt Him: out alone in the desert at night: the tremendous mystery. And that's just why I don't believe all your neat little dogmas and formulas about Him. To anyone who's met the real thing they all seem so petty and pedantic and unreal.'"[17]

That's how many of us in our pre-Christian phase used to feel about faith and particularly about the Christian faith. We thought we understood about faith when we absolutely did not. Even though we'd only superficially observed it, we had come to feel that faith was this thing that we already knew about in some deep, wise and intimate way that had set us above everyone else. We thought that faith was something we had stumbled upon while watching a sunset or whacking a golf ball, and we thought that the secret of it - the thing that we got about it while all the others didn't - was that there really wasn't anything to clutch at or to be understood about faith after all. It was just something to marvel at and that was enough. So we wandered around being bold in our imagined wisdom, saying things like, "But isn't that sunset awesome? There's something of God in there, you know."

All anyone has really done by reenacting that hackneyed and overrated scenario is to have made an occasional gasp at the majesty of God's Creation. His deliberate intent in giving us Creation in the first place is that it should serve as a concrete *tangible* to introduce us to the "immeasurably more" the faith-life holds in reserve for us. So it isn't faith, or the understanding of it, just because we recognize the universe as God's handiwork. It's a tiny glimpse at part of the work of the Faithful One, and a very small part at that. That isn't faith, it's the universal experience by which God intends to activate and direct our faith. It's a signpost pointing toward the rationality of faith.

The Stuff of Faith

Faith has substance and effect. Faith is more real than the most vivid reality you have known. You have enough of this primal faith lying dormant within you to propel you into the experience of the divine, because it has been planted within you as a gift,[18] every bit as much as God's grace is a gift, but you must use it. Once you've begun doing that you'll be much better qualified to talk about what's real and what is not. But you must take the risk and you must make the effort.

Lewis later comments on the statement of the R.A.F. officer by saying, "You see, what has happened to that man in the desert may have been real, and was certainly exciting, but nothing comes of it. It leads nowhere. There is nothing to do about it. In fact, that is just why a vague religion - all about feeling God in nature, and so on - is so attractive. It is all thrills and no work: like watching waves from the beach. But you will not get to Newfoundland by studying the Atlantic that way, and you will not get eternal life by simply feeling the presence of God in flowers or music. Neither will you get anywhere by looking at maps without going to sea. Nor will you be very safe if you go to sea without a map."[19]

Faith Abusers

Nor will you get anywhere near God without the exercise of your faith. Using your faith is work, and faith when used does work. Faith is intentional and difficult, but will produce amazing, rewarding results. As we exercise and properly direct our faith, it grows.

Jesus spent quite some time dealing with the abuse of simple faith, sometimes even in the "best" of his followers. I say it is the abuse of faith because faith is something we all possess, and we all misuse it when we fail to wield it toward the discovery of God.

At least four times Jesus used a pet name for the members of his ministry team. When he said *"O ye of little faith,"* he was actually saying *"You Littlefaiths!"*[20] Notice he didn't say "You Nofaiths!" Jesus knew they had faith because he had put it there when he created them. Only once did Jesus say anything like, *"Do you still have no faith?"* [21] In that instance he was really chiding his closest friends as if to say, "What will it take for you to recognize the faith that I have given you and to wake up to it? Are you still committed to acting as if you have no faith at all? Are you dedicated to *living your life out of its proper context?*" We are, you see, made to be people of faith.

Creepy Little Doubts

One day as Jesus was going about the work of his early ministry he received visitors from John the Baptist. If you know anything about The Baptist, as we often call him, you know that he had developed a large following as he preached to the people, urging them to "prepare the way of the Lord." John was an effective prophet, a true historical figure mind you, who served as the herald of the Messiah.

But then John ended up in prison and languished there for several months, inactive and physically excluded from the main flow of things as Jesus himself rose to prominence. The spotlight faded for John and discouragement naturally set in. John sent two of his followers to Jesus to ask him the question, *"Are you the one who was to come, or should we expect someone else?"*[22]

John's doubts, fueled out of proportion by his inactivity (doing nothing is the hardest thing there is on faith) got the best of him, even though Jesus would say, *"I tell you, among those born of women there is no one greater than John; . . ."*[23] We doubt, too. Our lives are steeped in doubt. Doubt masquerades as prudence, as wisdom, even as courage, although it is none of those. We think if only we had more evidence of God we might believe in him and follow him, but Jesus knows us.

To the faith abusers he said, *"[You're] like children sitting in the marketplace and calling out to each other: "We played the flute for you and you did not dance, we sang a dirge, and you did not cry."*[24] In other words, "You won't play a happy game, or a sad one. You won't believe one way or another. You won't use your God-given faith to embrace me with a reason or with a sign or with a miracle or without."

That's why we *must* play Let's Assume, remembering that God has already given to us the faith to do it. It may be severely corroded, but it is there and it can be hooked up and it will work.

Back to Our Original Faith

Lewis, again, gives us a good idea of how to perceive this. He's actually talking about something else, but I like to apply this thought to the way we all may come to recognize the faith within us and use it to get in the spiritual game. Lewis is referring to the Holy Trinity, which he terms the "three-personal Being." It's a difficult concept for anyone, but then it's equally as difficult to imagine the idea of a working personal faith when you've never used it before.

"You may ask, 'if we cannot imagine a three-personal Being, what is the good of talking about Him?' Well, there isn't any good talking about Him. The thing that matters is being actually drawn into that three-personal life, and that may begin any time - tonight, if you like." (Just as your journey of personal faith may begin in the same way right now, *if you like*.)

"What I mean is this. An ordinary simple Christian kneels down to say his prayers. He is trying to get into touch with God. But if he is a Christian he knows that what is prompting him to pray is also God: God, so to speak, inside him. But he also knows that all his real knowledge of God comes through Christ, the Man who was God - that Christ is standing beside him, helping him to pray, praying for him. You see what is happening. God is the thing to which he is praying - the goal he is trying to reach. God is also the thing inside him which is pushing him on - the motive power. God is also the road or bridge along which he is being pushed to that goal. So that the whole threefold life of the three-personal Being is actually going on in that ordinary little bedroom where an ordinary man is saying his prayers. The man is being caught up into the higher kinds of life - what I call *Zoe*[25] or spiritual life: he is being pulled into God, by God, while still remaining himself."[26]

That is precisely descriptive of our faith. Personal faith is required to seek God and to know God and to function in the realm of having fellowship with God, but it is also given by God, sustained by God, and fueled by God. Faith is demanded by God, but fully provided by God, yet it still remains that your allowing it and your participating in it is necessary for it to work at all. Later we'll learn that we're all infected with original sin. Just as equally, however, I believe we're infected with the antidote, and that is the latent seed of *original faith*.

You've Got It

The whole life of faith is actually going on within you this moment, waiting to burst into full motion at God's command, once triggered by the permission of your will. This is to be faith toward the greatest Good applied toward the supreme Purpose of God for your life. God begins his passionate appeal to win your heart by asking, "Doesn't such a faith as this *entice you*? Wouldn't you like to go along with it?" I challenge you to test it out. I can only hope that despite the speed bumps, despite the requirement of faith to play this game, you'll still choose to participate. Why not risk a little in order to gain infinitely more? Go ahead! Get past the faithbumps and get onto the open road.

Chapter Six
The Three Trees

Playing the Game

We now have returned to the concept of the game. The premise is simple: In order to hear and give proper attention to God's passionate appeal to win your heart you must at least temporarily accept some underlying assumptions. Once you have accepted them, you will have cleared away the rubble standing in the way of giving God's passionate appeal to win your heart a fair, complete and uninhibited hearing.

The Three Essential Assumptions

We will begin with what I have termed the Three Essential Assumptions of Christianity, and you will find them at the start of what I call The Clear Path Home. "Home" is the experience of God in all truth, beauty and eternity. The Three Essential Assumptions are like three large oaks shading the path.

I did the earliest and largest part of my growing up in a neighborhood called Bretton Woods. As you can imagine by the name there were quite a few trees around, and our yard had several. But there were three, perhaps eight feet apart, which had been planted side-by-side in a straight little row at the edge of an old-fashioned stone patio. My brother and I always called them "the three trees."

I have wonderful memories of slinging long ropes we had made by braiding binder twine we had gotten from my Uncle Gene's farm over the lower branches of the three trees. We would make a Tarzan swing or a great sailing ship with masts and rigging or a flagpole or some sort of fort out of them. We'd say things like, "Meet me out by the three trees," or "the three trees are the safe zone." Those three trees together made a sure landmark.

The three trees were something that you could see from a distance and know where your house was. They were a place you knew so well that nearly forty years after you had moved away you would still remember the stuff you had carved into them and where. You can still sit beneath them, even if just in your memory, and smell the same smells and flick at the same black ants that crawled on your neck. They were solid, those three trees, and they will grow forever. That's what the Three Essential Assumptions are like. If we meet there we'll know we're starting down the clear path home. And as we pass beneath their canopy they'll open us up to every spiritual possibility. They'll be our sentinels, our guides and our helpers.

Don't Get lost

Remember, an assumption is based upon solid reason and has the expectation of being proved true at the outcome. These assumptions are safe. They will prove true at the outcome, and I will reference a number of excellent works to which you may refer at a later time, [see Appendix A] but I urge you at this critical juncture not to get lost in having to prove, irrefutably and scientifically, these essential assumptions. That sort of approach is usually the weak point in our potential journey all the way to the end of the Clear Path Home. We get back on a sidetrack and never get off and therefore we never get home. That is not to infer that the essential assumptions comprise a sidetrack. Pursuing them to distraction, however, does.

For our purposes here, let's start down the path under the shade of the Three Essential Assumptions, and let's finish the course. Let's Assume that there are answers to any questions which pop up along the way regarding any of the assumptions. Let's Assume that the answers will be logical, well founded, and both intellectually and spiritually satisfying. Let's Assume that they will be very good answers indeed for careful, thoughtful and intelligent people. Let's Assume they will be such good answers because they in fact will be. If you will trust me on that, then once we've walked The Clear Path Home you can go back and explore any side issues that you like, to your heart's content. I will help you by providing good places to discover solid answers. Fair enough?

We will define each core assumption by identifying some of the satellite assumptions attracted to it by the force of its gravity. We will also consider some additional assumptions, but the first three are the essentials. The others are sound, but often are later discoveries in one's walk of faith within the Christian context.

The First Essential Assumption

God is. Let's Assume there is a God.

This assumption should not stretch us even as far as my earlier statement about the whole world being in the grip of the evil one, because approximately 95% of us believe in God. Approximately 72% of us believe him to be the omnipotent, omniscient, perfect Creator of the universe and consider him to be not only alive today but also actively engaged in ruling over the universe.

Actually, nearly nine out of ten of us say God created the universe. This is becoming an increasingly popular position as the scientific discoveries of the unbelievable odds against life having originated and evolved by chance mount up. The odds are simply too astronomical.

I'm not a betting man, although I do say, "You bet!" a lot. (Apparently I assume that others bet a great deal.) But as I understand it, if the odds of a horse winning a race are only 1 in 10 to the 42nd power, the better wager is that there will not be very many players stepping up to the window and saying, "I'll take that bet!" Common sense assumes that God is, and he is eternal. He is the Uncaused Cause, who has brought about everything else in creation, both material and spiritual. God exists, as the Scripture puts it, *"yesterday, and today, and forever."*[27]

So, Let's Assume there is a God and that he is making a personal appeal to you that is worth your hearing. Let's Assume that he is the "three-personal

lled him; Father, Son and Holy
ce, expressed as three distinct
indivisible. The three-personal
ke.

...cted with this assumption, let's say
... of Nazareth is the second Person of this three-personal Being and that he came to earth 2,000 years ago as God incarnate (that is, God embodied in human form) to communicate with us and to accomplish something very important on our behalf.

Let's Assume that Jesus was a real historical figure, fully God and fully man at the same time, and that his historicity is satisfactorily documented, including the fact of his alleged bodily resurrection from his actual physical death by crucifixion (being nailed to a cross which was then stuck in the ground until the victim died). We're assuming that Jesus lived and died just as the Bible and other reliable historical documents say he did.

Let's Assume that God is the Creator and the Sustainer of the universe and everything in it. We're accepting that the purpose of Creation is not only to provide you with an environment for living, and mankind with a platform for playing out its existence, but also to introduce you to the idea that this grand Creation does indeed have a Creator. Life's play has an Author, someone who is infinitely wiser, more powerful and morally superior to you and me. Someone to whom we innately know we must, in the end, submit.

Let's Assume that God has both a personal interest in you as a unique individual and a personal plan for your life. Let's Assume that *"God is love"*[28] and therefore loves you, and that he has plans for great hope and a wonderful future for you, even if you haven't discovered those plans just yet.[29] Let's Assume that he wants to communicate his interest, his love and his concern to you, and that he wants to enable you, to strengthen you, to care for you and to accompany you through every challenge and every blessing that you will ever encounter. Let's Assume that he is a relational God who can be touched by our infirmities[30] and that he is neither unreachable nor aloof. Let's Assume that God in the person of the Holy Spirit is inexplicably near to you and that he is in fact reaching out to you right now.

The Second Essential Assumption

God has spoken. Let's Assume God has allowed us significant insight to his reasoning through his written Word, the Bible.

Regarding the Christian Bible, 60% of the adults in America today agree, to some degree of intensity that, "the Bible is totally accurate in all of its teachings." The Bible itself is the best-documented piece of historic literature in the history of the world, not to mention the all-time best seller. Let's Assume that the Christian Bible is truly the Word of God. Let's Assume that it is a widely supported, thoroughly documented piece of literature. Let's Assume the Bible has been inspired by the Spirit of God, written according to his instructions, and divinely preserved intact through the ages, remaining inerrant in its original manuscripts and miraculously effective in achieving its unprecedented intent.

Let's Assume that the content of the Bible is true, and that the theological, doctrinal or conceptual difficulties certain passages present for some individuals can be intellectually and emotionally satisfied. Let's Assume that through the Christian Bible God speaks.

Let's Assume that the Bible is the only piece of literature in the history of the world claiming to be superior revelation that passes the historical, scientific, archaeological, philosophical, experiential, practical, intellectual and prophetic tests altogether, all-in-one. *The only one.* Further, Let's Assume that it does so with brilliant flying colors. Aren't these assumptions fun? Remember, at the end of it all we must be able to substantiate them. My anticipation is up, how about yours?

Let's Assume that the deepest thinkers and the most ardent critics of the Bible and the Christian faith can, by enactment of even the slightest and most sensible bit of personal faith, become the staunchest defenders of the Christian Bible. They can, and have, become believers with a capital "B." Believers of the unswayable sort, champions of that which they previously misunderstood and maligned. Let's Assume that there is a dynamic within what we intrepidly call The Word of God that stimulates men and women to have confidence in it, supernaturally calling them to rely upon its principles to guide their daily living. It is a dynamic that must repeatedly be denied in order to be beaten down rather than followed.

The Third Essential Assumption

God can be known. Let's Assume God can be known by placing one's faith in Jesus Christ, and since God has required faith, he also has provided it to each of us

While 95% of American adults believe in God, 85% identify themselves as being "Christian" in their faith. Intriguingly, 63% of us have no idea what Jesus' most vivid allusion to salvation, the verse John 3:16, refers to. As an encapsulation of the gospel message, John 3:16 may rank as the highest and best. That the large majority of us don't know that verse could be a problem, even though we agree that God can be known, and we may do so through faith in his Son Jesus Christ. We may desire to know God, but apparently we have done very little to fulfill that desire.

Knowing God is an audacious yet entirely attainable possibility. He can and will be known in a reciprocal and intimate association. The Scripture reveals one key when it challenges us to *"Come near to God and he will come near to you."* [31] Jesus gave us a picture of this potential relationship in one of his prayer sessions with his Father. *"Now this is eternal life: that they may know you, the only true God, and Jesus Christ, whom you have sent."* [32] *"Righteous Father, though the world does not know you, I know you, and they* [those of us who have faith in Christ] *know that you have sent me. I have made you known to them, and will continue to make you known in order that the love you have for me may be in them and that I myself may be in them."[33]*

This is not the picture of a God who desires to remain aloof and unapproachable, but one who can be known and who knows all about us. He has lived here as a man, so he has fully experienced the challenges of this life. *"For we do not have a high priest who is unable to sympathize with our weaknesses, but we have one who has been tempted in every way, just as we are - yet was without sin."[34]* This is a God who can be known, and the experience is worth the investment.

Chapter Seven
The Corpus Conclusion and Other Safe Assumptions

Jumping to the Corpus Conclusion

There is another thing we may safely assume, although it is less essential, if that is possible, than the three trees. Let's Assume that the Church is actually the *Corpus*, the Body of Christ. What is more, Let's Assume that the Body is not all messed up, crippled, or deformed, but is instead alive and whole and well. That may be difficult imagining, because whether from the outside or in we hear so much to the contrary.

We hear that the Church is compromised today. We hear that people have mucked it up, and there are even these ideas out there that it has apparently gone beyond Christ's control, that it is irreparable, irredeemable. If you know anything at all about the *Corpus*, you know better than that. We must give the Church the benefit of the doubt, or I should say we must give the Church and its Head the benefit of our faith.

It Belongs to Jesus

Jesus took total responsibility for the Church. I used to serve as the pastor at an inner-city-type church that my wife and I planted. Several times each year I would hear a report from my wife about the children she works with at the elementary school. One of them would say, "Isn't your husband the one who owns that church over there?" We always had a fantastic laugh about it because the last thing any pastoral minister does is to own the church he serves. I would think that in owning something you would not only have the responsibility for it but you would also occasionally be able to get it to do what you want!

Enough said. The point is that even the professional or vocational ministers do not own the Church. Christ owns it, lock, stock and barrel. And he has assumed all the responsibility, all the authority, and exercises all the prerogatives.

One day Jesus and his team had come into the region of what today is called the Golan Heights. It was a particularly pagan area, with the shrine to the Greek god Pan being located there, among many other pagan influences. Jesus looked around that enclave of infidelity, taking it all in. Then he turned to his group. "What are people saying about me? Who do they say that the Son of Man (his favorite title for himself) is?" he asked.

The group had several answers. "Some say you're John the Baptist. Others think you're Elijah or Jeremiah. Maybe one of the other prophets."

Jesus looked over the unlikely troop, knowing that one day this motley batch of men would become both wise from God's wisdom and brave from God's encouragement and would become the spiritual leaders of the human race. He smiled a bit at the prospect. Then he engaged them directly. "But what about you?" he pressed. *"Who do you say that I am?"*

One of his lieutenants who usually went by the name of Simon Peter stepped forward speaking otherworldly words. "You are the Christ. You're the Son of the Living God!"

Jesus approved. "You're a very blessed man, Simon son of Jonah. This wasn't revealed to you by any human means. It's a message straight from my Father who is in heaven. And I'll tell you something more. You're Peter, and we all know that means "a small piece of a much bigger rock." But the truth you just uttered is like Gibraltar. It's the massive foundation of God's truthful revelation. It's the truth upon which I am going to build my Church. The gates of hell will not be able to hold out when assailed by this truth, nor will this truth cave in when all the powers of hell mount their attacks against it. That's how significant this knowledge is, and that's how powerful my Church shall be."[35]

He Tells No Lie

This is important. Jesus tells no lie, so Let's Assume that Jesus always has done and continues to do just what he said. He has built his Church. He is the overseer of his Church even today. The Church is as Christ intends it to be. It is alive and well, watched over, nursed and nurtured, inhabited by Christ. The Church is still giving birth, bearing fruit and having influence on the world today.

"I will build my Church," Jesus said. He does it, he has done it, he will do it; the Church is his.

Advancing, growing . . . losing, reduced to a remnant . . . feasting or in famine, favored or despised in the eyes and understanding of men. A dragnet load of good treasures, beloved sons and daughters, and unworthy intruders all existing together, for now, as God has chosen to allow; the sorting out will be done at the end.[36]

The Church is well and the Church prevails. Two thousand years ago Christ began his building and it continues today. He is building. He remains the Cornerstone, the Architect and the Builder, as well as the Preservationist. In his Church losers win, and those who are of no repute rise up to lead. In his church the despised are cherished, the languid become energized; the shortsighted receive God-given, God-inhabited, God-sized vision. Let's Assume this all is so and that God uses imperfect people. He pours himself into cracked pots and in the pouring all the fissures are healed.

So? So the message and the mission of the Church remain true. Within its walls you will find truth, even though it seems you must strain to see it. Yes, you will also find hypocrites and the spiritually lethargic, but still, somewhere within this Body, you will happen upon its Builder, even though there are some personalities who may try to get in your way. God sustains the Church. The baby has never been thrown out with the bath, nor will it ever. Upon the rock of this safe assumption you are invited to rest.

Let's Assume: Life Answers May Be Expected

"Then you call on the name of your god, and I will call on the name of the LORD. The god who answers by fire-- he is God." Then all the people said, "What you say is good."
1 Kings 18:24 NIV

Now I know that the LORD saves his anointed; he answers him from his holy heaven with the saving power of his right hand.
Psalm 20:6 NIV

Everyone who heard him was amazed at his understanding and his answers.
Luke 2:47 NIV

The prayer of a righteous man is powerful and effective.
James 5:16 NIV

Here is another healthy assumption: The God of Christianity is known as the answering God, so answers may be expected. His answers are considered more than just pertinent to life; they become its guiding force and substance. Let's Assume there can be a God-reaction to your pleadings. Let's Assume there is logic for your incertitude. Let's Assume there are rejoinders to your questions and even to your accusations. Let's Assume that your petitions rouse Heaven.

So your asking can be satisfied by your receiving, your seeking could be rewarded by your finding, and your knocking may be appeased by God's opening up. Your invitation for God to come down will be accepted, and conversely, your presence will always be welcomed in Heaven's throne room. You will always make the roster of God's team, and you will always be a starting player, *if* all of that should become your sincere desire.

The dynamic driving this assumption is simply that of expectation. Let's Assume you may expect a return on any investment you make in God. If you invest your hope, its fulfillment will be returned. If you invest your trust, you will gain an inheritance. If you invest this temporal day and your earthly future, you will be repaid by the standards of eternity.

A Pledge of Simplicity, But No More Than Possible

Let's Assume that we will discover the clear path to fulfilling all of our expectations through the course of our study, but also that the elements we will weigh all are vital to our consideration of this process.

The problem with many attempted commitments to Christ and the Christianity that he has authored is that they are made frivolously or from an ill-informed level of understanding. When that happens, the outcome is understandably disenchanting. There are certain things you must know about coming to Christ, or the result will be that you will not have come at all, or you will have come to some "christ" other than he who is eternal and supreme.

We'll attempt to be simple, but Let's Assume that we are weighing only the basic, irreducible essence of the Truth about the Christian experience. It may be something a bit more ponderous than you would like, but as Einstein said, "Things should be as simple as possible, but no simpler."

I'll assume this: Here you are on Truth's doorstep, and finally you are willing to take a serious look at the guts of Christianity. You want to turn over the potential Truth of Christianity as it stacks up against the spiritual "whatever" you've been entertaining up to this point. You're going to give it a fair hearing and a good effort. You're going to put aside your preconceptions or what you're sure you "know" about God, being open to the idea that you just might hold some misconceptions. Will you allow all of that, for the sake of hearing his appeal to win your heart?

The Triple-Dog Dare

Let me ask you to do something huge, if you dare. Let me ask you to put a bit of that latent faith to good use right now. Remember, this is about your faith, not mine, so let me ask you to assume that you have that seed of faith we have discussed, and let me challenge you to use it. *If you dare*, why not pray this prayer:

"God, if you are truly there, please reveal yourself to me. Reveal the way of Truth to me as I submit myself to this process of investigation, consideration and introspection. I am taking this first step, and as I do it I am asking you to respond . . . your Spirit to my spirit. I'm waiting expectantly for your response, God. Right now that's all that I can do."

Chapter Eight
The Intense Drama of Your Willful Heart

No English

I watched in amazement as the professional bowler loosed the ball. At first it curved to the left, then abruptly swerved to the right, then gracefully back to the left as it approached the pins. What English! I have no English; not in tennis, not in table tennis and not in bowling. None whatsoever. I propel the balls and they fly straight. Sometimes, in tennis and ping-pong, they fly very low and on a good day very fast, but always very straight.

Straight has its benefits, but it also has its drawbacks. In bowling, for example, I can often hit my mark, which in general is that little pocket between the head pin and the next. But without English to spin and throw those pins on impact, I've got to hit it perfectly. When I do, it's beautiful, and sometimes I get in the groove and it's strike, strike, strike. But other times I'm off, and even if it's only ever so slightly, the pins just won't fall. I throw a lot of splits.

My wife, Pat, on the other hand, has very interesting English. Once, when we were first married, we went bowling with some good friends. Pat went to the line and took her aim, but when the ball left her hand it shot backward and not forward, and the only things scattering were Wayne and Nan, I and the people behind us. We were . . . in awe. We gaped. The people in the lanes on either side of us gaped. The whole bowling crowd fell to gaping in startled, silent, yet oddly reverent amazement. The jukebox wound mournfully down, sounding as if a tiny little jet had crashed into it. The lights flickered and went black for just an instant.

Then, slowly, everything wound back up. The gaping left us, but not the amazement. Never had anyone in the history of bowling ever missed the mark so badly. They never patched the hole that she put in the wall. That was thirty years ago, but my wife remains a legend in those parts to this day. Or at least that's the way I choose to remember it. My wife is famous. She set a new standard for missing the mark.

The Wrong Mark

In the Scriptures we read about the tribe of Benjamin mustering an army. Among the troops were seven hundred valiant Benjamite warriors *"who were left-handed, each of whom could sling a stone at a hair and not miss."*[37] It must be nice never to miss your mark, even when it's only a hair's breadth wide. That's perfection. Unfortunately, these extraordinary marksmen chose the wrong targets. They attacked their own countrymen in one of history's most woefully regrettable and wrongheaded wars. They may have hit the mark every time, but it was the wrong mark and they were hitting it for the wrong reason.

That's the human condition when we live outside of a relationship with Christ. We're not perfect, most particularly when it comes to our behavior. We cannot hit God's behavioral standard. We do not hit the mark of right living. If we think we do, in the end we discover we have chosen the wrong mark in the first place.

We should know, although many of us don't, that we all are sinners. The overriding image of what we call "sin" when it is depicted in the Bible is that of "missing the mark."[38] It is to be off target both in the negative and the positive sense, so that sin is not merely missing the right mark, but it is purposely taking aim and hitting the wrong mark.

There are other biblical definitions of sin in the old and new testaments: bad or badness; wickedness; guilt; iniquity; err; wander away; rebel; evil; godless; unrighteousness; lawlessness; transgression; to be [perhaps willfully] ignorant; to go astray; to fall away; hypocrite. Sin comes in many guises. Scripture indicates that we are fully aware of each of these types of sin, and engage them all with complicity. God's mark or standard is completely visible and is clear to us. We miss it then, or commit sin, with full possession of our faculties, and thereby we incur guilt for sinning.

I Don't Like My Sin

We're naturally resistive to this idea of personal sin. We really don't like it, although some feel considerably less responsible for their sin than do others. And there are always the extremes. Some people are steeped in guilt over every breath of a sinful thought. They usually are the sort of people who think if they would just "try harder to be gooder" they'd be able to get this thing down all on their own, but they are less common than those who totally deny their sin and their sinful nature, or those who pretend that they're comfortable with it.

The Lady Who Never Sinned

I started college a bit late in life. I was twenty-five and already had a young family. Two of our children had been born by that time. I left a job as a line supervisor for General Motors, moving my family from Lansing, Michigan to Converse, Indiana so I could attend Marion College, which is now Indiana Wesleyan University. Being the hard-driving know-it-all that I was, I decided I was ready to take on a post in pastoral ministry at the same time I began my ministerial studies. I was called to a tiny church in a very small town, and there I began cutting my shepherds' teeth.

One day I went visiting, making pastoral calls on a few individuals who were loosely affiliated with the congregation. You did stuff like that back then, particularly in a small town. I wanted to meet them, hopeful of persuading them to pick up the pace of their attendance, or at least give us a single try. One visit in particular is framed in my memory.

It was a beautiful summer day in early August. It was pretty hot, but a cheerful sun lazed across the crystalline blue sky. There wasn't a hint of a cloud. It had been a great season, with just the right balance of rain and sunshine and gentle breezes for the crops to flourish. Everything was a verdant green. That afternoon I stopped at the old farmhouse on the edge of town. A widow lived there, and she was eager to talk. We sat at the 1940's vintage kitchen table, sipping ice-cold sun tea.

"I have a bone to pick with you about that church, preacher," she said. "I'd come to services more often, but it offends me too much to see what's going on there, and I'm afraid people will get the wrong idea." She pursed her lips, tilting her nose a bit higher in the air. "I'm afraid they'll think I approve," she sniffed.

My heart had started to creep up into my throat. I was truly puzzled. There were just a few precious people in the congregation at that point, and as far as I knew we were all getting on famously. I was pretty sure I was preaching "the old-fashioned gospel in the old fashioned way," so I couldn't imagine what sinful thing we could possibly be harboring. There just wasn't enough going on for something to be out of hand. We had a few women and a couple of children to make up the whole crowd.

"I'm not sure I understand," I stammered.

"Well, you probably don't know it yet, so you might not be to blame. But one of those women who takes up the offering has been . . . *divorced!*"

"Divorced?" I repeated dully.

"Oh yes, she certainly has. And a divorced woman has no business ever doing anything in the church! So I can't go there until it gets settled properly."

"But, don't you think she's been forgiven for that?" I was about to get my first lesson in tiny town, small church doctrine.

"Well I don't know about that. I don't imagine so, but that's not the point."

"What is the point?" I wondered aloud.

"Even if she's forgiven, she can't parade herself in front of the whole town doing the Lord's work. We must exhibit higher principles than that. At least I certainly must." I sensed the point was nonnegotiable, but had to try anyway.

"We've all sinned, and we all stand in need of God's forgiveness. He tells us to forgive one another and to love one another, just as he has forgiven us and loves us. We're supposed to understand how forgiveness and restoration work themselves out by practicing those things in our own lives and in our church." Her eyes grew wide and she sat up straighter yet.

"What?"

"The Bible says that we all have sinned and fall short of God's standard. We've all messed up and offended God in some way. By your way of thinking none of us would be worthy to pass the offering plate."

A Very Dangerous Idea

It was as if you could hear my words slapping this poor dear lady across the face. Her head wobbled and then snapped back for an instant as livid purple indignation plastered itself all over her features. Part of me felt guilty for the assault. Eyes wider still, she spat, "I've *never* sinned!"

I was startled at her statement, and I thought I had misheard. "Pardon me?"

"*I've never sinned.*" She hissed the last word, the "s" word, disdainfully. I sat wonderingly, in open-mouthed curiosity. I'd never met a perfect person before. I suppose it should have been a sacred moment. I truly did not know what to say.

A bird chirped in the distance, and the ancient oscillating fan whirred a quiet whir, punctuated by the soft clattering of the metal blades. Outside, the porch swing creaked gently back and forth in the light breeze. We held at that impasse, that lady and I, pretty much for the remainder of my tenure at the church. I don't remember how I disengaged from that specific visit, but I'll always remember it as a mental caricature of how much we can rebel against the idea of personal culpability for sin.

We may deny our sin totally, as that lady did, or we may rationalize our sin away, comforting ourselves with the sentiment that everyone does it, and so many do so much worse than we. Look at Hitler, or Stalin, or Pol Pot, for goodness sake. Look at Saddam Hussein or Osama Bin Laden. Look at that drunken, malingering, wife-beating, child-abusing pedophile across town! Personal sin? Give me a break. Mine's not any worse than anyone else's, that's for sure.

Chapter Nine
The Clean Room

Clean Rooms and the Cleanroom

How good do you suppose you'd have to be to impress God with you goodness, so much so that he'd want to share intimate fellowship with you? Let's think about that for a bit.

God has a behavioral standard that defines his holiness, his purity and his righteousness. It is the standard of perfection. Anyone willfully, and therefore knowingly, violating that standard cannot have fellowship with God. He will not compromise his holiness just so he can carouse about singing, *"I've got friends in low places."* His absolute purity is offended by sin.

We had a tough time with a couple of our kids keeping their rooms clean. So when they achieved the state of "clean" it was always quite an event. I always used to play the critic when they were done with their rare cleaning adventures. They'd come and get me, and they would be so proud, but they also would be giggling expectantly because they knew what would happen. I would feign disbelief and a couple of heart attacks, but then I'd get down on my belly on the floor and root around under the bed or somewhere until I came up with a miniscule piece of lint. Then I'd hold it up and proclaim loudly, "Aha! I knew I'd find filth in this room!" Then they would usually beat me up.

There is a different type of clean room, however, which has to do with certain manufacturing environments. A "clean" bedroom wouldn't even begin to compare with a clean cleanroom.

In the manufacturing cleanroom we worry about such things as skin particles, or dust from clothing or shoes, or even bacteria from the human body. If you're preparing to enter the cleanroom, you'd best take care of bodily functions before you decontaminate and dress in cleanroom clothing. One instruction list cryptically cautions, "It is impossible to correctly blow a nose in a cleanroom." Then check out some of these garbing requirements:

- The left cuff and left zipper can be taken in the left hand and the right zipper and the right cuff in the right hand. The coverall can then be gathered up at the waist and one leg placed into the garment and the other leg into the other, without the garment touching the floor. By releasing one cuff at a time, first one arm and then the other can then be placed into the garment.

- The garment should then be zipped all the way up to the top, with the yoke of the hood being tucked inside the collar.

- If the garment has snaps at the ankles and wrists, then these should be snapped shut.

- The crossover bench should be crossed over now. This bench is used to demarcate the slightly soiled changing-zone from the cleaner entrance zone and allows cleanroom footwear (overshoes or overboots) to be correctly put on.

- Personnel should sit on the bench. One leg should be raised, the cleanroom footwear put on, the leg transferred over the bench and placed on the floor of the entrance zone. Footwear should be put on the other foot and the leg taken over the bench. While still sitting on the bench, the legs of the cleanroom garment and the footwear should be adjusted for comfort and security. Personnel should now stand up.

You get the picture, and as you might guess, we could go on and on citing regulations and procedures. Still, with all of these precautions, cleanrooms regularly suffer contamination. They must undergo frequent decontamination.

God's Cleanroom

Clearly, heaven is God's cleanroom. It is his holy environment, and nothing unclean will ever enter in. No unclean, unholy, sinful person will violate or contaminate God's cleanroom. If such a person were to somehow enter heaven, God wouldn't have to flop down on his belly and root around to find the filth. It would be appallingly evident. What's worse, God's holiness and purity would consume the unclean one instantly, because all of these attributes of God are self-protecting.

"To the Israelites the glory of the LORD looked like a consuming fire on top of the mountain."[39]

"For the LORD your God is a consuming fire, a jealous God."[40]

"Therefore, since we are receiving a kingdom that cannot be shaken, let us be thankful, and so worship God acceptably with reverence and awe, for our God is a consuming fire."[41]

Catch a glimpse with me of the New Jerusalem, as we sometimes refer to heaven:

"I did not see a temple in the city, because the Lord God Almighty and the Lamb are its temple. The city does not need the sun or the moon to shine on it, for the glory of God gives it light, and the Lamb is its lamp. The nations will walk by its light, and the kings of the earth will bring their splendor into it.

On no day will its gates ever be shut, for there will be no night there. The glory and honor of the nations will be brought into it.

Nothing impure will ever enter it, nor will anyone who does what is shameful or deceitful, but only those whose names are written in the Lamb's book of life."[42]

No Compromise

God is love, and the intensity of his love for you is unfathomable by the human mind. Yet there is an aspect of God's own nature that he loves more than he loves even you. In coming to know God and in growing deeper in our intimate relationship with him, many people fail to recognize this, but *God loves himself more than he loves you!* God loves his own holiness, his purity, and his essence *more than he loves you.* Thankfully so, for if God conducted the management of his own personality by our human standards, we would have him compromising it all the livelong day. If there is anything about God that I must know is constant, it is his moral superiority.

God's purity is inviolable. He will not compromise it, even for you. His holiness is unapproachable by sin. We cannot conceive of how fierce are the fires of God that protect his essence.

God has an inviolable sense of justice, too. Sin is harmful moral pollution. It is rebellion against a perfect, loving and righteous standard, and it hurts other people as well as smiting and saddening God. And God takes our personal sins personally. All sin, by God's way of thinking, is to be considered as being committed directly against God, no matter who was hurt in the process.

When David, the king of Israel, had sinned by having sex with Bathsheba, who was another man's wife, then tried to cover it up by engineering her husband's death in battle, in the end he expressed a healthy understanding of the nature of all sin. In Psalm 51 he said to God, *"For I know my transgressions, and my sin is always before me. Against you, you only, have I sinned and done what is evil in your sight, so that you are proved right when you speak and justified when you judge."*[43]

A Fair Wage For A Day's Work

There are some hard facts about sin that you should know. Sin breaks God's moral law and therefore must be punished. God is holy, righteous, loving and just. He doesn't compromise one personal attribute just to appear "better" in the next. God's justice demands that all sin be judged and fairly compensated, just as he does with all righteousness.

The murderer, the rapist, the thief, the thug, the con artist, all will come to justice in the end, definitively, completely and finally. So will the slanderer and the merciless old gossip sitting on the back row at church.

Actually, when we think about this, we're fine with it. We would think much less of God if he compromised his justice, because we all want justice to be done.

The Bible characterizes the commission of sin as earning a wage. Sin's wage is death, and wages are an obligation that must be paid off. Sin's wages must be paid because God's fair and universal law decrees they must. It is written: *"... the wages of sin is death."[44]* It is also written, *"Now when a man works, his wages are not credited to him as a gift, but as an obligation."[45]* So the obligation rightfully due to a man or woman who works the works of sin is that he or she must be paid the wages of death. That death, while ultimately physical, is more substantially spiritual. It is the separation of the individual's soul from fellowship with its loving Creator.

Some of us, in fact the majority of us in America today, believe that we will deflect the wages of our sin if we do at least enough good things to outweigh the bad that we have done, or else because God is a "softie" who won't really follow through on his promise of eternal justice. Fully 99% of American adults believe that they will not go to hell when they die, even though, as I mentioned previously, the majority of us do not possess a basic understanding of the means of salvation! It doesn't work like that.

EXTRA: "Man Jumps to the Moon!"

The gap between our unrighteousness and God's holiness is huge. Imagine that the distance is the same as that from the earth to the moon, and that in order to bridge the gap you must make the jump. Imagine all of the obstacles blocking your way, such as the earth's gravitational pull, no atmosphere between here and there, the unthinkable climate of space and all of that.

Imagine that in order to be united in fellowship with God you must jump from the earth to the moon and you must do it on your own. Your only vessel will be your body and its only propellant will be your natural strength, your good deeds, and the fact that you are a "nice person." Throw in the facts that you do a lot of good reading and that you have an excellent education. For the purposes of this scenario, let's award you a doctorate in whatever subject you like. Add to that your very sincere expectation that God isn't serious about judgment.

If you keep yourself in perfect shape, and you follow a perfect diet and a perfect strength-conditioning program, how much higher toward the moon can you jump than the next person? How much higher are you able to jump because you have done good deeds? How much higher when your jumping is hyper-fueled by your niceness? Add your education in now. How much higher? Add a distinguished career, a huge net worth and your sacrificial financial and physical support of a hundred great causes. Give yourself a Nobel Prize, too.

Now go to the highest point on the face of the earth when, during the orbiting and spinning of these bodies, it is at its closest to the moon. Now how much higher can you jump toward the moon than the next guy? Take a running start. Are you getting a foot higher? Two feet? Perhaps it's four feet. I really don't know, but let me ask you this: How much closer, relatively speaking, does your extra four feet in jumping, even from the highest point on earth, get you to the moon? On a properly scaled representation would the separation between you and the next person even be discernable? And how close would either of you come to reaching your goal?

The fact is you both would come crashing back to the earth, held captive by the force of gravity. You both would fall miserably short in your attempt, when the only thing that counts is actually making it. How much closer one is than the other has no bearing on the whole business whatsoever when the point is getting to the moon and neither of you has made any notable progress.

Sin is the stopping force, sin is the obstacle, sin is the anchor, sin is the deal-breaker, and sin means your trajectory is sorrowfully off the mark. Then comes the kicker, that even if you should, by an enormous human miracle, make it, the cleansing, purging, swallowing fire of God's holy presence would either bounce you back, as a force field would, or simply consume you.

Chapter Ten
The Terminal Vortex

Warning!

Our receptors pick up many warnings as we go through this life. We all know the story of the infamous McDonald's "WARNING: HOT!" label on every coffee cup and the scalded victim turned millionaire who inspired it.   Now nearly all products have warning labels. The pharmaceutical advertisements on television lately really irk me. The content of the warnings is far greater than the substance of the ad, and the announcer's voice always drones on in that annoying, conspiring undertone, talking about potential hair loss and nervousness and incontinence and such. Have mercy!

One toilet bowl cleaner used to carry the warning on its container: *"Safe to use around pets and children, although it is not recommended that either be permitted to drink from toilet."*[46] We never had a problem with our pets doing that, but on a hot, sweaty day you just couldn't keep the kids out of the toilet bowl. You know how that is, right? (Okay, I'm kidding. The pets drank out of it, too.)

We receive many warnings pertaining to sin as well, but somehow we just can't keep ourselves away from it. We can't stop drinking from the bowl.

We are warned through Scripture, and through the bitter experience of those who have preceded us, that sin is an enslaving force, taking us captive as its prisoners. Sin is a taskmaster, getting us in its merciless grip and refusing ever to let us go.

We are warned that sin is a thief, stealing our time, our talents, our strength, wealth and youth. We are warned that sin eats up our resources as well as our dignity. Sin erodes our very personhood.

I call sin "the terminal vortex." It's a powerful, swirling, hungry and turbulent force, sucking in everything around it. Once swept into its powerful clutches we become sin's property. We relinquish our freedom, we relinquish our rights, and we are owned by sin. Jesus said, *"I tell you the truth, everyone who sins is a slave to sin."*[47]

The Hook in Your Nose

Body piercings are now appearing in what seem to me to be the strangest of places. We stopped at a restaurant the other day and I have to admit my dumbfounded curiosity got the best of me, so I spent much of my attention watching a young man with the most interesting stuff stuck through his skin that I've ever seen. I was particularly taken with the silver bone poking through just beneath his lower lip. I think it was a tiny femur, but who can be sure? I wasn't comfortable asking, "Hey! Is that a femur in your chin?"

In the Bible we read the story of a wicked king who ruled over Judah, and who ended up with a nasty body piercing for himself. Manasseh did all sorts of evil things that were explicitly forbidden by God. He built places for worshiping foreign gods. He constructed altars to worship the "starry hosts" in the very courts of the Temple of God, and then bowed down to them there. He sacrificed his sons to pagan gods by fire, and practiced such detestable things as sorcery, divination and witchcraft, and consulted mediums and spiritists.[48]

All of these things were anathema to God, and ultimately the penalty for his sin caught up with Manasseh. In an incredibly symbolic occurrence the king was taken prisoner. His captors *"put a hook in his nose, bound him with bronze shackles and took him to Babylon."[49]* Manasseh lost his freedom, his dignity and any sense of control over his own life. The controlling effect of sin was vividly illustrated in the captivity of poor Manasseh as he was humiliated, stripped of possessions and power, and finally led by the hook in his nose.

The Great Human Disaster

Humanity controls its own affairs and does so stubbornly independent of God. Whether we're Creationists or Darwinists or something in between, we all must come to that same conclusion. Humanity has decided to go it alone. If majority rule has anything to do with it we have taken our position, we have chosen our fate, but there's a hook in our nose.

In 1894 an English teacher included a note on Winston Churchill's prep school report card. It said, "A conspicuous lack of success." Churchill rose above his inauspicious beginnings to become a powerful leader. When it comes to the performance of humanity in managing the universe the same pronouncement may be made over us as well. The evidence shows nothing but "A conspicuous lack of success." The real concern, however, is that unlike Churchill we don't seem to be rising above it.

Crashing Icons All Around

Regarding the ship Titanic, one employee of the White Star Line was quoted as saying, "Not even God himself could sink this ship." Indeed, Titanic was universally regarded as an amazing tribute to man's scientific and technological ingenuity. Titanic symbolized man's ability to tame and command his environment. Titanic made him the master controller of the elements, at least until overconfidence and an iceberg took her down.

Similarly, Challenger and Columbia were American Supersonic Transport Shuttles. The whole world watched, aghast, when Challenger was destroyed on takeoff. When Columbia disintegrated during its attempt to re-enter Earth's atmosphere on February 1, 2003, President George W. Bush could only say, "It's gone. There are no survivors." One of the doomed shuttles was coming and the other was going, but coming or going we couldn't avoid or control these heartrending losses. Coming or going we were vulnerable then and we are vulnerable now.

On three separate occasions I have stood at the rim of Ground Zero in New York City, the sight of the World Trade Center attack on September 11, 2001. On the first occasion, in early January of 2002, the rubble still was around one or two stories high.

I will always remember later that night as I stood looking back at Ground Zero from the observation deck of the Empire State Building. From the gaping hole in the lower Manhattan skyline where the Twin Towers belonged, two giant shafts of light beamed heavenward, the smoke from the still smoldering debris filling the shafts and the whole effect creating two ethereal but poignant memorials. Two towers of smoke and light replaced the concrete, steel and glass in the place where people should have been.

The second time I stood at the rim was the next April, and the wreckage had been brought down to ground level. The third time was that June, and it happened to be the day that the subway was uncovered. Later the work paused and workers and observers alike bowed respectfully as the remains of several of the terrorists' victims were carried out. It was hard to process. There was no way to assimilate the feeling because what caused it never should have happened, and such a feeling does not belong in the human spirit.

At one time Minoru Yamasaki, Chief Architect of the World Trade Center, had said, "The World Trade Center is a living symbol of man's dedication to world peace." Apparently the symbolism was lost on some.

Richard Nixon, Michael Milken, Enron, Internet startups, Martha Stewart, all disappoint us. Terrorism, subversion and fear destroy any sense of peace. Riots in Los Angeles, California and riots in Benton Harbor,

Michigan express our unrest and our rage over the state of this world.

Middle America, Too

I can see the same effect as I look around my neighborhood in Middle America. We live in what Time Magazine has named one of the Top Ten American Small Cities to undergo economic transformation. We have reinvented our city and now are prospering.

My wife and I, however, have chosen to make our home in an area that is the secret sin of our city. We live in Meadows, which is our very own miniature urban inner city. We have 330 homes in our development, accommodating approximately 1,200 people mostly locked in lower middle to lower-class poverty. This community flies in the face of our prosperity.

Daily I see children running, often late into the night, unsupervised and uncared for. Improper clothing and poor nourishment, neglect, abuse, apathy, hatred, self-inflicted ignorance, disdain for authority and absolute selfishness are the order of the day in my community. Attitude, attitude, attitude, everywhere you look. Oh, there are exceptions, thankfully; points of hope and light, great and solid families, but they are unique in our neighborhood.

I have a neighbor who tells his wife, "You're really lucky I do drugs, because if I didn't, I wouldn't work. I go to work because that's where I can get drugs, and that's where I can get the money to pay for them." We do what we can, with God as our sustaining strength, and after eight years we have seen some wonderful transformations. But too few, too few. We have been involved in a truly cross-cultural ministry, but even after all of these years I feel as if I don't yet speak the language of our neighborhood. It is the language of despair.

I look at my community and I see my neighbor riding proudly on the bow of the Titanic, crying out at the top of his lungs, "I'm king of the world!" And I often feel our grand experiment must look like a terrible failure, although I know it's not. Not yet. Not ever when so much as one family has been helped, even though every tiny step forward is a tremendous battle. Still, there are times when humanly speaking I'd like to pack up, move out and say, "It's lost. There are no survivors."

Enough Inadequacy to Go Around

The icons of humanity's greatest achievements, the leaders of our governments, our top financiers, and the results of our loftiest and most ideological social experiments seem invariably to reflect our deepest inadequacies. They fail. In these failures we see the fragility of human life and our undeniable vulnerability.

Titanic sinks and we're reminded how subject we are to pride and stupid bravado and how susceptible we are to our own poor planning. Challenger and Columbia disintegrate and we remember that, going or coming, we don't always learn from the past and that our best attention to detail is not always enough. The

World Trade Center and the Pentagon are attacked and our faith in our amazingly potent economic engines and the world's most powerful military machine collapses right alongside the towers.

We abruptly realize that the underpinnings of our society aren't settled on a foundation quite so unshakeable after all. The terrorist attacks and the fall of Enron and other corporate giants reveal and underscore our failures at brotherhood, world peace and even simple morality and ethical behavior. When it comes to failure humankind has written the book, and has really nothing left at which to fail. We have run the gauntlet and covered the gambit.

What's the Devil's Due?

We know that we are the children of God, and that the whole world is under the control of the evil one.
1 John 5:19

The great dragon was hurled down - that ancient serpent called the devil, or Satan, who leads the whole world astray. He was hurled to the earth, and his angels with him.
Revelation 12:9

One of the heads of the beast seemed to have had a fatal wound, but the fatal wound had been healed. The whole world was astonished and followed the beast. Men worshiped the dragon because he had given authority to the beast, and they also worshiped

the beast and asked, "Who is like the beast? Who can make war against him?"
Revelation 13:3

In all fairness, we have had some powerful help in creating the Great Human Disaster in which we live. The Bible says the whole world is in the grip of the evil one. That's not too much of a stretch for any of us to imagine, although only approximately four to six out of ten adults in America today (depending on which survey you accept) believe that Satan is a real, living and powerful being.

We don't necessarily need to give the devil his due in this regard, however. Though the world is indeed in his grip, we seem to be quite prone to handing it over. He hasn't had to do all that much to get our goods. We own the concept of haphazard spirituality, and display a certain sloth over spiritual things and a resulting unguardedness concerning our spiritual intake.

Spiritual Soup

Again, I see this as I look around my own community. Interestingly enough, I see it most in the religious atmosphere. In our miniature urban inner city (and incidentally, these little urban models exist everywhere, even in the tiniest hamlets) we have a microcosmic reflection of the religious cultures of the world and of its history. We have a strong contingent of New Ager's, for example, whose life approach is reflective of ancient eastern mysticism, Confucianism, Hinduism and Buddhism and isn't particularly new at all. This gets mingled with the pop psychologies of Dr. Phil and Dr. Brothers and Dr. Ruth and of course Dr. Oprah, America's leading "theologian." That is then seasoned with all the other spiritual opinion sets floating around on the airwaves and ooching their way into our minds.

These concoctions are comprised of the spiritual gassing off of movie and rock and rap and sports and news and business superstars, and the writers and producers and directors and promoters and spin masters who create and sustain them. The spiritual ideas of our newly digitalized, media-shaped world aren't all that hard to pick up on, since they're terribly overt and are promoted ad nauseum anyway, and they don't require much thinking at all, which may account for our ready acceptance.

The Church du Jour

Spiritual roots have essentially rotted away, too. Another disturbing trend in America today is for people to attend the Church du Jour. Some families have two or three or even more "home churches." Which one they attend on any given Sunday depends upon which of their felt needs is crying the loudest for attention and how well the given church does in meeting that need.

They have become quintessential spiritual consumers, going to this one for great soul-soothing music, this one for an intimate small group environment, and that one for the best pump-me-up sermons. Whichever ministry has the best deal going or most effectively scratches where they are itching is where they will attend, but they can just as easily sit out for several weeks or months or years when they're not facing any particular crisis, feeling no loss whatsoever.

Who You Gonna Call?

The saddest effect from consuming this spiritual soup, however, is that the New Age of post-modern enlightenment or the haphazard occasional drive-by churching of oneself doesn't see us through the wickedness, hurt and difficulty that daily living so typically and so often deals out.

When the chips are down you can't just waltz in and talk with Oprah, no matter that your life has fallen in the gutter. She's not taking your call. She can't see you today. Nor can the other pop-theologians. Doctor Phil, even though he sometimes says some great stuff, can't visit you while you're dying, reassure and guide you when you're terrified, or look after your loved ones when they need it or after you're gone.

The real answers and the rubber-meets-the-road-for- the-long-haul authenticity we crave in this life just cannot be derived from pop-theology, nor will the prescription we pick up at a random church service work when we take such tiny, irregular doses. Smoke and mirrors, my friend, nothing but smoke and mirrors. I've personally picked up the wreckage of shattered human lives far too many times to hold any other opinion.

These are products or methods or approaches to spirituality that we have self-constructed and they are not representative of God or his divine plan, purpose and provision for your life. They all miss the mark. It's like feeding only sugar to your soul. Empty calories produce lots of fat, and ultimately diabetes.

Chapter Eleven
The Frog Lied

The Prevaricating Amphibian and Me

"Now the serpent was more subtle than any beast of the field which the LORD God had made. And he said unto the woman, Yea, hath God said, Ye shall not eat of every tree of the garden?

And the woman said unto the serpent, We may eat of the fruit of the trees of the garden: But of the fruit of the tree which is in the midst of the garden, God hath said, Ye shall not eat of it, neither shall ye touch it, lest ye die.

And the serpent said unto the woman, Ye shall not surely die: For God doth know that in the day ye eat thereof, then your eyes shall be opened, and ye shall be as gods, knowing good and evil."

Genesis 3:1-5

Nearly everywhere I look in my home I can see a frog. My wife is very fond of frogs, although that does not include any real ones. I don't think she'd ever touch a real frog. The other day I inadvertently hacked a great gash in a hapless frog as I mowed along a landscaping tie where he must have been hiding. I immediately informed Pat the frog lover, but she never made even the teeniest attempt at providing first aid. His little corpse is rotting out there still today. Well, actually I think I mulched him later. No, Pat would never touch a real frog, but the collectible sorts have a thriving colony going at our place.

Once when we made a trip to New York we were walking through Manhattan and spied a large bronze sculpture, perhaps four feet high, of a leaping frog. We decided to get a photo of my wife kissing the frog. Our friend Jenny was with us that time. Jenny teaches Art to middle schoolers, so she's a creative type. She got a brainstorm and had me stand directly in front of the frog sculpture in roughly the same pose the frog was striking. My wife then kissed me for another photo. So now we have the frog being kissed and the very, very handsome prince coming along after. It's a great set of pictures, particularly the second one.

This Fable's for You

Whenever I look at those photos I'm reminded of the fable. Princess meets frog, they converse, and the frog reveals that he's in fact a prince who has been placed under a curse. The princess, you will recall, had somehow to find enough strength of stomach to kiss the frog, but when she did the frog was transformed into her prince. Yahoo!

But then there's the twisted version. The princess kisses the frog, and the frog remains a frog. The princess is repulsed as she realizes the ugly truth. She's been taken. The frog lied. The lecherous amphibian just wanted to kiss a beautiful maiden. In the worst version of the fable, the princess gets warts on her lips and gradually morphs into a toad herself.

That image is perfectly descriptive of what Satan has sold the human race and how sin has affected us. We have given in to nothing but lies resulting in the gradual destruction of our humanity. We become prisoners to the utter erosion of the image in which we were made. The frog lies and the human race is left wrecked in the bargain. His hook is in our nose, but it can take some doing to recognize it.

Stealth Sin

This is the age of Fourth Generation Warfare, or 4GW as it has come to be known. The first generation included smoothbore muskets and men maneuvering in line and column. The second generation came with the rifled musket, breechloaders, barbed wire, machineguns and indirect fire. The motto of this fighting generation was, "The artillery conquers, and the infantry occupies." The idea behind it was conglomerated firepower versus conglomerated manpower.

Then came the third generation. This saw the birth of significant tactical refinements. An army might, for example, allow penetration but then turn the enemies' momentum against him.

Now we have the fourth generation. In this new generation combat is dispersed over a wide area. The battlefield is less defined, and the delineation between war and peace is often very vague. It has been called "nonlinear conflict," even to the point where the battlefields and the fronts are indefinable. Often, the distinction between military forces and civilians disappears.

There are vast differences in the culture of war today versus preceding generations. In the past there was profound emphasis on drill, marching in ranks, saluting uniforms and such. It was a "culture of order." Terrorists have defied all of that, and are particularly adept at working from the inside out in a free society. Terrorists use the freedom of free countries, our strongest asset, against us. They can maneuver from the inside of the free society while at the same time being defended by the rights of the democracy itself. They end up being protected by the laws and civil processes of the society they are attacking to destroy. This has birthed a warring culture of disorder.

While the weaponry of the organizational-minded military is impressive, with Hummers and Blackhawks and Stealths, the terrorist has invented weaponry "unplugged." The trunk of a car is loaded with powerful explosives and is turned into its own form of stealth bomber, indistinguishable from any other car on the road.[50] A child is trained in Jihad and indoctrinated in self-destruction for the greater good of the angry cause, or of the angry god that spawned the angry people behind it. (I heard it well said the other day "Angry gods make angry people.") Then she is rigged with explosives and becomes a walking warhead, often more sophisticated and accurately destructive than a computer-driven smart bomb.

Things are not the same. These are not our grandfathers' battles any longer. It is difficult to find any sense of "honor" in war anymore. The ideas behind it are more abstract, subversive and diabolical than anyone ever could have imagined.

The New Sin

I propose that a new generation attitude toward personal sin has infiltrated the fabric of our American society right along with the terrorists who are attempting to destroy us. I call it "stealth sin." It is an attitude that works through us from within. It is an attitude with which we are born, but one for which we have lost the remedy. This attitude of stealth sin gives birth to a mindset that actually denies the existence of sin, except when such a term is convenient for labeling people we don't like. It is an attitude that condemns any idea of the existence of absolute moral truth, and actually calls such ideas a lie.

To capture the erosion of our spiritual sensibilities today, I defer to the Scripture once again. I think our nail gets hit squarely on the head with this one.

"Woe to those who draw sin along with cords of deceit, and wickedness as with cart ropes, to those who say, 'Let God hurry, let him hasten his work so we may see it. Let it approach, let the plan of the Holy One of Israel come, so we may know it.'

"Woe to those who call evil good and good evil, who put darkness for light and light for darkness, who put bitter for sweet and sweet for bitter.

"Woe to those who are wise in their own eyes and clever in their own sight." [51]

Hey! It's Not All That Stealthy After All

The attitude of stealth sin attempts to disguise itself by dressing up in the rags of the new tolerance, and portraying itself as the new, excusable, even endearing Sin-Lite, but I believe it deserves to be called out. Sin-Lite and the new tolerance are lies.

These ideas hold the position that all ideas and behaviors must be tolerated, and preferably embraced, since the enlightened mind understands that there cannot be any such thing as absolute moral truth.
Rather, what is true for you is fine for you, even though it may not be the best idea for me. But out of respect, I'll probably try it on because we're both decent and intelligent human beings and it makes us feel warm and fuzzy to affirm one another. So I will tolerate anything, except, as it now goes without saying, that which harms another person. Or animal. Or tree.

But I hear revealing voices out there. They are the satirists who claim to speak for America today, but they're cluing us in on a dirty little secret. They're not so righteous themselves. One of these guys preaches his message of disdainful intolerance from a lofty self-constructed platform, *"Born again? No, I'm not. Excuse me for getting it right the first time."* *"God's got more phonies claiming to know his will than Howard Hughes."*

Another adds his fuel to the fire, *"Can't we silence those Christian athletes who thank Jesus whenever they win, and never mention his name when they lose?"*

We'll Tolerate Anyone . . . Except for YOU!

The new tolerance is actually saying, "I will tolerate all ideas except one: If some hapless fool should assert that there is, after all, absolute moral truth out there somewhere which serves as a fixed, guiding principle, and worse, should that same hapless fool further assert that someone else has violated this absolute moral truth, the fool will immediately be branded as intolerant and will be identified as the worst sort of sinner imaginable."

So, there are no sins or sinners any longer, except for those who say there are sins and sinners, which would be the commission of neo-sin, I guess. Anyone daring to hold to such an archaic idea as the existence of sin and sinners is judging others, and therefore must be judged. He will be ridiculed, he will be tortured, he will be hated and if at all possible, at least in character, he will be assassinated. Such an intolerant, presumptuous bigot will not be tolerated! How dare he hold an idea about what is right and what is wrong, much less have the gall to promote it. That's wrong. He's wrong! How dare he judge another? Off with his head!

You know, I'm wondering if you're picking up on my sarcasm here, because I've been working pretty hard at it, and it's nice when your efforts are at least recognized, if not appreciated.

Our Own Dirty Hands

In rendering these judgments of someone else's perceived "intolerance," have we not dirtied our own hands? Have we not displayed our own hypocritical nature by engaging in the very practices that we so eagerly censure?

"Excuse me for getting it right the first time." Oh please. So are you saying that you alone are therefore qualified to judge and ridicule and condemn and are immune from recrimination when you so freely, frequently and incessantly do it?

"Phonies!" Really? Are all Christians phonies? Can you so authoritatively and categorically condemn and dismiss the largest faith community in America? Are Christians the only class besides trailer trash today that it's just fine to vilify, to smear and to hate?

"Can't we silence those Christian athletes . . ." As one of Annie's friends so aptly observed in the movie, "Oh my goodness, oh my goodness!"

Is it really OK to wonder, *"Can't we silence those Christians?"* Is that really the sentiment of your heart? Is that your true nature showing through? And once we've silenced those Christian athletes, just whom will we be silencing next?

I know Christianity has its hypocrites. There are psychopaths who do whatever nastiness they do in the name of Christianity. Just as there are psychopaths who do their equal nastiness in the name of animal rights and world peace and ecology and Islam and following Charles Manson. There could be a nut out there just being his psycho self in the name of Jello for all I know.

There are psychopaths everywhere, and they're all equally psychopathic, but intelligent, healthy and rational human beings do not use the psychopaths as the qualitative measure or the definitive statement of any particular movement or belief system. We still eat Jello.

Satire or Bigotry?

Once again, let's call this attitude what it is. It isn't harmless satire, it's sinful bigotry, and it is meant to manipulate the minds of the masses. Just because we incorporate a destructive idea into a standup comedy act doesn't make it harmless or right. Just because we're free to do so and it makes us sound hip doesn't mean we should.

This is simply the same voice of hypocrisy that emanates from any sinful disposition. If we're the ones singing this song it puts us in the same category as the worst religious bigot or the sleaziest unprincipled televangelist we can name. The Bible calls it what it is, revealing the bitter core of human nature that is buried within each of us. Are we not the literal fulfillment of the Scripture, which sees us for who and what we are apart from God's healing, forgiving, restoring grace?

"You, therefore, have no excuse, you who pass judgment on someone else, for at whatever point you judge the other, you are condemning yourself, because you who pass judgment do the same things."[52]

The Worm From Within

These attitudes and the resulting actions shouldn't surprise us. They are the evidence of sin, and sin comes from within. We all are born with a disposition toward sin. We are, in a sense, already caught in the terminal vortex at birth, while at the same time when we are old enough we willfully cast ourselves into it, anyway.

It's interesting to me that one of the most common worms plaguing apple growers, the coddling moth larva, doesn't mount its invasion from the outside. Rather, the adult parent lays eggs inside the apple blossom. The blossom turns to fruit, the apple grows and one day the larva is hatched, deep inside of the fruit. It begins its life cycle by eating its way out of the apple.

It's that way with our original sin. Our parents, Adam and Eve, laid the egg of sin within us, so to speak, by the damning choice that they made. We are cursed with their curse, which includes pain in childbearing, the tilling of rebellious ground by the sweat of our brow, choking weeds, but most disastrously spiritual and physical death.[53] We are separated by this spiritual death from our loving creator, and, consequently, have sin seeded into our disposition.

It's Not My Fault!

The natural inclination is to lay the blame for our sin on someone or something else. For example, we might blame Adam and Eve themselves. After all, they started the whole thing. Or perhaps we should blame El Diablo. He did the tempting. It seems he was the mastermind of the subversive plot. Or God. We could blame God because he didn't superimpose his superior will and quell the terminal vortex when it was just an infant sand devil, before it could kill anybody. He didn't step in and stop Mephistopheles before we sold him our souls.

Anna Russell wrote a poignant song that she titled *Psychiatric Folksong:*

> *At three I had a feeling of ambivalence*
> *toward my brothers,*
> *And so it follows naturally*
> *I poisoned all my lovers.*
> *But I am happy; now I've learned*
> *the lesson this has taught;*
> *That everything I do that's wrong*
> *is someone else's fault.*[54]

Well, that's the gist of it. We all have chosen to sin. We all are bent on sinning. The wages of sin is death, and sin's wages will be paid; they must. While humanity has had thousands of years to get it right, we're not gradually improving. We're caught up in the same quagmire, sucked up into the same terminal vortex. Sin, that lying old frog, is having its way with us. Perhaps we'd ought to find a way to mulch it.

Chapter Twelve
Buzz is Broken and I Can't Help

A Broken Buzz

I dug out the movie *Toy Story* last night and Pat thought I was crazy, since none of the grandchildren were here, but I had to check out this illustration. Do you know that movie? Woodie and Buzz Lightyear. Buzz is the new toy with a towering superiority complex. Buzz is not just any toy. He wears a space suit, but he's not an astronaut, he's a Space Ranger, with years of academy training and tremendous weaponry built into his extreme environmental space garb. Most amazingly, he's got wings built into this suit, and he can FLY! What's more, Buzz isn't just hanging out, he's on a major mission at the bequest of Star Command. He's a one-man, universe-saving, dive-bombing arsenal.

When Buzz comes on the scene with the other toys, he's absolutely certain that he's a one-of-a-kind. They may be toys, but he's Buzz Lightyear, Space Ranger! Through a series of missteps and silly events, Buzz and Woodie, the affable and down-to-earth cowboy figure, find themselves next door at Sid Phillips' house. They're being held captive by Sid, the kid who likes to mutilate and blow up toys.

Buzz is undaunted by all of this. He's strong and brave and in control. He's leading the charge to make an escape. He's dodging Sid's nasty Pit Bull, when he runs into a room where Sid's dad is asleep in his easy chair, with a beer in his hand and the TV blaring in the background. Then a powerful voice breaks in and urgently intones, "Calling Buzz Lightyear!" Finally! Star Command has at last responded to him on this strange planet where he thinks he's crash-landed.

But then Buzz sees that it's nothing but an advertisement. It's a commercial for Al's Toy Barn, and down at Al's they have hundreds of Buzz Lightyears. Miserably, they're even on sale. They're not Space Rangers, they're plastic toys. Buzz begins to realize that his sophisticated built-in gauges are nothing but stickers. His voice fabricator is just a cheap little toy recording. His laser destroyer beam is just a tiny red light. And his wings, of all things, his wings . . . the commercial even says it: *"Not a flying toy."*

Buzz walks out of the family room in a state of shock and dismay, treading with heavy, sad steps all the way to the upstairs landing. He is totally dejected, but then has this one flicker of hope. *Those things* are toys, but not he. Maybe they're replicas of him, but he's the real deal! So he climbs to the top of the wrought iron banister, and he sees an open window in the stairwell. This is no time for messing around, so, snap! Buzz deploys his wings, and with little hesitation takes a mighty leap. He's Buzz Lightyear and he's going to fly right out of that window and save the world!

Buzz sails into the air in perfect form. His expression is fixed and determined, but then things slip into slow motion. You can see the agonizing, chilling realization set in. Buzz isn't flying, he's falling, and he's not even doing it "with style." There's nothing within him to power his flight, and all of the junk he's wearing, even the weight of his own body, is just pulling him down. His expression fades, his eyes narrow, and grimness covers his features. Then Buzz crashes, and it isn't pretty. One of his arms comes off, and as the camera pulls back you see Buzz lying there in a heap on the bottom step, looking up at his arm dangling over the edge of the next step up.

Buzz is broken. He can't fix himself. He's not the savior of the universe. He's not the almighty. He needs help.[55]

The World's Worst Acting

History's worst television ad has to do with an emergency alert system for seniors. There is a gizmo that can be worn around the neck with a panic button on it. If you have an accident or succumb to an illness and can't reach the phone, you simply press the panic button and it sends a message of some sort to the monitoring service. Help is dispatched and you are saved. The production is bad, the acting is bad, and the scripting is bad. The focal line is, "I've fallen and I can't get up." It is so bad that it defines badness, I'm sure, up and down Madison Avenue. Except for one thing: You still see that ad, over and over again. It is aired relentlessly, and that can only be for one reason. It must work.

One has to ask, with such corny production values, why is it so effective? Because this scenario really happens. Elderly parents and spouses fall, and they can't get up. They need help and it's sometimes out of reach, or at least we feel it might be. So that's our mom on the floor. Or perhaps it's us, calling out for help.

That's life, and that's spirituality. Buzz or bad-acting mom, we're all lying in a heap on the floor, and we're all lousy actors, trying to cover it up, trying to force ourselves to feel invincible, whether we can see ourselves that way or not. We have been wrecked by sin.

What If I'm Not OK?

Once a long time ago I met with an alcoholic. "Blake" was in a bad way. We had an appointment fairly early in the morning, and we were to discuss the possibility of his participating in a recovery program.

The instant I saw Blake I knew we had a problem on our hands. It had actually become a fairly predictable scenario for me, having worked with more than a few alcoholics. His face was as red as red gets, and the sweat was literally dripping off of him. He smelled bad.

If you've ever been around a whiskey alcoholic on the "morning after," you know the smell I'm describing. It oozes out the pores, the irrefutable evidence of a recent bender. When we got to my office I closed the door for privacy, and the stench nearly drove me out. I couldn't wait to end that interview.

Blake didn't have a problem, though. According to him, the comedy of errors that made up his current life situation was the fault of several other people and a couple of unfortunate coincidences. Blake was in total denial, and still at least partially under the influence; enough so, in fact, that he really felt he was charming and believable as he wove his pitifully transparent tale.

We chatted about his condition, and I asked, "Do you have a problem with alcohol?"

"No, I really don't believe I do. I've never had any problem stopping when I have to. Sometimes I go out and get drunk with the boys, but lots of people do that. I usually go out and have a couple at lunchtime, but I'm not alone. Once in a while I drink at work, but I'm not the only one who does that either!"

"So, you're telling me that even though alcohol apparently has enough of a grip on your life that you go out and drink on your lunch break, and it affects your judgment enough to cause you to take a drink while you're on the job, you still don't have a problem?"

"That's right. I don't have a problem."

Over time Blake was confronted with reality and with the fact of his stubborn denial. It took a while, but I eventually began to see the signs of a breakthrough in Blake's reasoning. A few tears fell, and the realization began to solidify in his mind. He was at least coming to the point of asking himself the critical question, "What if I'm *not* OK? What if I do have a problem? What if I've just been denying it all these years?"

***

Solomon says we are all prone to making such misjudgments about our own condition, but God sees through them, and their consequences can be terrible.

"Every way of a man is right in his own eyes: but the LORD pondereth the hearts." "Most men will proclaim every one his own goodness: but a faithful man who can find?" "There is a way which seemeth right unto a man, but the end thereof are the ways of death."[56]

Solomon's father, David, says that, left to ourselves with no outside influence, we downright refuse to acknowledge our sinfulness.

"An oracle is within my heart concerning the sinfulness of the wicked; There is no fear of God before his eyes. For in his own eyes he flatters himself too much to detect or hate his sin."[57]

A Window on Your Soul

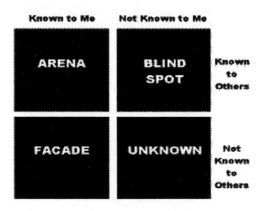

108

The Johari Window is a very popular model portraying an individual's level of self-awareness and communicative ability. It basically deals with the patterns of information processing between others and ourselves. A square divided into four equal sections represents the interaction of two primary sources of information, namely, Self and Others.

Area One is the information that you and I both know. It is called the Arena. Area Two represents those things I know about myself but have not made known to you. It is called the Facade. Area Three is my Blind Spot. It holds those things of which I am unaware about myself, but which you plainly see, yet have not communicated to me. Area Four applies to both of us, and it is the Unknown. It contains things that neither of us has recognized, but which are nevertheless true about me.

Take a look at the Arena with me, and perhaps we can better understand the Johari Window. The Arena of my life is an important area of shared information. It is that which both you and I know to be true about me. It is said that the information known by me - known by you largely controls the interpersonal productivity of our relationship. The more you know about me, and the more I know you know it, the better our communication becomes, and the more productive our relationship.

The Arena is where good communication takes place, so the larger my Arena becomes, the more productive my relationships with those I've allowed to step inside. As my Arena grows larger in our relationship, my Facade shrinks, my Blind Spots shrink, and the Unknown dissipates. I think this is why good marriages always get better over time. Self-disclosure is a process, and it occurs best under conditions of acceptance and mutual respect.

My wife knows things about me that I never would have foreseen revealing to another human being, yet she loves me without exception. I love her all the more because of her faithful and loving response in my Arena. She carefully enters dialogue with me about my Blind Spots, and successfully undertakes to enlarge my Arena through that dialogue.

On the strength of our relationship, I value my wife's input, be it revelation or affirmation. I crave her feedback when I speak in public, because she can recognize the nuance of a bad attitude that may have flavored a particular statement. She hears the message as others hear it, with an objectivity that I cannot muster up by myself. Because she truly knows me, Pat also hears the message *better* than others hear it, so her critique is the most valuable.

Blake's problem resided in the Blind Spot category. He likely felt it was behind the Facade, although there's a small chance it might have been in the Unknown. That's unlikely, based upon what I observed in him that he did not know for himself. Others helped him discover the reality, pulling the whole thing out into the Arena.

But What About You Today, My Friend?

Let's Assume that you may have blown it. Let's Assume that you may have a Blind Spot, and it just might be sin. I'm praying right now that the Holy Spirit will communicate that to you. Would you be willing to drop your preconceptions about your spiritual condition before God and ask the question of yourself, as you've never asked it before, "What if I'm *not* OK? What if I'm caught in the terminal vortex of sin, and I don't even feel the pain or anticipate the consequences?" Well? What if?

Not long ago I sat down with my boss and had a chat about a tedious process of self-discovery I have come through over the past three years. That process was painful - hideously so at times. At a certain point in your adult life, as you grow into maturity, you quit focusing on your potential and start looking candidly, analytically and ruthlessly at your accomplishments. I had been doing that for a protracted time, and I didn't like what I saw.

I learned, through healthy feedback, I think, that a number of qualities I had and fancied to be strengths weren't really appreciated all that much by others. In fact, some of my perceived strengths were being interpreted as weaknesses, and that was right. I had some foundational flaws in my style, and even in my character, that needed to be both healed and corrected. It was a tough, tough journey that continues today.

After I had recited this litany of self-awareness and pain my boss looked at me and said, "You know, it occurs to me that you are probably the healthiest right now that you've ever been. When you get to the point of acknowledging a need, that's the healthiest day of your life. Even though it may seem it's going to kill you, it's a banner day. The worst is behind you at that point, as long as you're committed to the rest of the journey."

The chorus of a Carole King song says,

And it's too late, baby, now it's too late, though we really did try to make it. Something inside has died and I can't hide and I just can't fake it[58]

We all get tired of faking it. Perhaps, with the help of the Holy Spirit working on your understanding, you've just stepped into the Arena about your sinfulness before a holy God. Perhaps you're communicating, at last, truthfully about your relationship, or lack thereof, with God. You're self-disclosing what he already knows about you, but the realization is for your sake, not his. You're simply offing a serious Blind Spot. You need not feel as if it's too late, by any stretch. Quite the contrary, it's just in time. This just may be the healthiest day of your life. Just don't fake it.

Chapter Thirteen
Life's Little Questions (LLQ's), or Life's Greatest Question (LGQ)?

Sin Grips

Sin gets a grip on our lives and never wants to let go. Our own remedies don't work. We really are beyond self-help. In the movie *Godfather III*, Don Michael Corleone manipulates and maneuvers to take the Corleone family out of the mob. After decades of the worst sorts of criminal activity, he finally wants to make all of their business concerns legitimate. He wants to cut the ties, but ends up lamenting, "Just when I thought I was out, they pull me back in!"

Licking the Blade that Bites Us

Sin certainly has that binding influence, but we also keep going back for more on our own. Radio personality Paul Harvey tells the story of how an Eskimo kills a wolf. The account is grisly, yet it offers fresh insight into the consuming, self-destructive nature of sin.

"First, the Eskimo coats his knife blade with animal blood and allows it to freeze. Then he adds another layer of blood, and another, until the blade is completely concealed by frozen blood.

Next, the hunter fixes his knife in the ground with the blade up. When a wolf follows his sensitive nose to the source of the scent and discovers the bait, he licks it, tasting the fresh frozen blood. He begins to lick faster, more and more vigorously, lapping the blade until the keen edge is bare. Feverishly now, harder and harder the wolf licks the blade in the arctic night.

So great becomes his craving for blood that the wolf does not notice the razor-sharp sting of the naked blade on his own tongue, nor does he recognize the instant at which his insatiable thirst is being satisfied by his OWN warm blood. His carnivorous appetite just craves more - until the dawn finds him dead in the snow!"

The Body of This Death

The Apostle Paul dramatizes the idea of sin's grip, calling it *"the body of this death,"* and conveying his deep anguish over ever being free from it.

"But I see another law in my members, warring against the law of my mind, and bringing me into captivity to the law of sin which is in my members.

O wretched man that I am! who shall deliver me from the body of this death?"[59]

Some scholars understand the phrase *"the body of this death"* to describe an ancient form of torture that some of the tyrannical despots of those days would inflict on certain victims. They would seize a living man and bind him with chains to a dead body. Virgil gives us the horrible, vivid picture as he describes the atrocities of the ruler Mezentius.

What tongue can such barbarities record,
Or count the slaughters of his ruthless sword?

'Twas not enough the good, the guiltless bled,
Still worse, he bound the living to the dead:
These, limb to limb, and face to face, he joined;
O! monstrous crime, of unexampled kind!
Till choked with stench, the lingering wretches lay,
And, in the loathed embraces, died away!

The putrid blood of the corpse would gradually infect the living body, bringing about a slow and terrifying death.

Adam Clarke comments, "We may naturally suppose that the cry of such a person would be, Wretched man that I am, who shall deliver me from this dead body? And how well does this apply to the case of the person to whom the apostle refers! A body - a whole mass of sin and corruption, was bound to his soul with chains which he could not break; and the mortal contagion, transfused through his whole nature, was pressing him down to the bitter pains of an eternal death."[60]

Life's Greatest Quandary

We have spent considerable time laying a foundation for the understanding and the ownership of our sin. We see its dominance in our individual lives and in the affairs of humankind. We recognize its enslaving disposition. We reap sin's wage, that remuneration which ultimately results in physical death, but worse, confines our souls even in this life to the netherworld of spiritual separation from the Creator God.

I've heard a lot of preaching through the years. Often, when an evangelist is characterizing the urgency of the hour and the lostness of humanity, he will speak of a world that is "lost and dying" in its sin. That really isn't the case. Unless we have been restored into relationship with God we have never lived. We came into this world as spiritual stillborns. We crave life and living, but we're dead. The Bible has told it as it is. Paul writes to the Christians in Ephesus, reminding them of their previous quandary,

"As for you, you were dead in your transgressions and sins, in which you used to live when you followed the ways of this world and of the ruler of the kingdom of the air, the spirit who is now at work in those who are disobedient.

All of us also lived among them at one time, gratifying the cravings of our sinful nature and following its desires and thoughts. Like the rest, we were by nature objects of wrath."[61]

You see, apart from Christ we're not lost and dying; we're lost and dead. We do not need to be found and nursed, we need to be found and resurrected. Those are two entirely different ideas.

Life's Little Questions

It's tough living as an "object of wrath." It's not what we want. No one enjoys living in the fallout of his or her failure, walking in the constant rain of retribution. At some point we recognize, with the help of the Holy Spirit, that we are being destroyed by the crushing consequence of our sin. That's a healthy, albeit frightening, realization.

With this understanding comes a frustrated desperation. Our perspective changes. Before this point, we majored in life's little questions and life's minor discomforts. But with this quickening of our consciousness to the graver, eternal matters of spirituality and life, those things no longer seem so important. They become more like the whining of an ignorant, overindulged child than the heretofore wise and weighty matters we once perceived them to be.

Perhaps we used to ask, "Who am I?" My generation was particularly fond of asking, "Where am I?" and then setting out to find ourselves. My wife and I graduated in the same class from the same high school. We remember at graduation standing and talking to one of our classmates. We were sharing our aspirations and our plans for careers and our relationship when he said, "Well, that's fine for you, but I'm leaving. I've got to go find myself." It was such a caricature of our day. We sometimes joke that as far as we know he's still out there looking.

It's nice to discover yourself, and to get a handle on your ultimate purpose, but when you realize you're bound to the body of this death the bigger priority is to get free.

Another of life's little questions that we may have asked up to this point is, "Where am I going?" It's really quite a hopeful question. We always hope that the answer will be, "Directly into prosperity and fulfillment! Into infamy and immortality!"

It's distressing, though, when you find your face pressed together with that of sin and death to hear that vile cadaver give us its answer, "Where are you going? Nowhere that you can control; only where I take you. Down with the ship! That's where you're going . . . down with the ship to rot and decay!"

The World Doesn't Have It

Please don't lose this focus. The world doesn't have the solution for us. We can see from its history that it doesn't know how to make itself better. The world can wound, but it cannot heal. We can sometimes, through great effort, prolong our lives, but we cannot save them.

Life's Greatest Question is not, "What must I do to improve myself?" Our understanding of the human predicament tells us we *can't* improve ourselves. We're doing our best, and our best just isn't enough. Our best effort isn't going to get any better than it is right now, not even if we could somehow muster up that hundred-and-ten percent that we so idealistically commit to giving as we strive our way through life.

Neither is Life's Greatest Question, "What must we do to combine our efforts and deliver ourselves by group effort?" Go team! But the United Nations can't do it. They may keep on trying, but even if we ever could manage to "all work together and just get along," our combined best efforts wouldn't be enough to fix our broken world, let alone save a single soul. We're just not that smart and we're not that good. Rather than believing in ourselves, we need someone bigger in whom we can trust.

We don't need what the world has to offer. We don't need a pep rally; we need the stark truth. We don't need a motivational speaker to inspire us and pump us up to give it our best and sweat it out. We don't need a self-improvement course; *we need a Savior.*

Life's Greatest Question

Yes, bound limb to limb to the body of this death, staring the corpse in the face, experiencing the creeping, invasive infection of sin as it oozes into our being leaves us no time and little room for philosophical debate. Raising only the little questions at a time like this constitutes fiddling while the Empire incinerates itself.

Instead we find ourselves, in the middle of the dark night, crying out from the urgent immediacy of our terminal desperation. "Wretched human being that I am! Who will deliver me from the body of this death? Tell me! Hear me! Help me! Anybody! Anything! *What must I do to be saved?"*[62]

"At last, at last," says the Spirit, "he's asking the right question. She's moving the right way. They're

asking Life's Greatest Question!   And soon they'll
discover it's not what they must do to be saved, *it's
whom they must trust.*"

Life's Ultimate Solution

Again, *what about you today, my friend?*   Have
you come to that point yet? Have you experienced the
crisis of the conscience regarding sin?" If so, you may
be ready for God's solution.

The imagery we have been pondering is stark and
difficult. It is repulsive and offensive. Our humanity
hates it and rebels against it. Perhaps you've even
had to put this aside for a period of time because
of your revulsion.   But that is the imagery of sin,
and it is impossible for its characterization to be too
strong. Those are the facts of sin, and they cannot
be overstated. The imagery is offensive, but no less
offensive than God's solution. In fact, it is not *nearly*
as offensive as God's remedy.

Chapter Fourteen
The Crux

A Scent of the Crux

When Mel Gibson's movie, *The Passion of the Christ* came out, it was preceded, accompanied and followed by a big flap over the whole idea. The film depicts the last twelve hours of Jesus' life, when he was arrested, tried, scourged, mistreated and finally crucified on a cross. It seems to me that this debate serves as a thoroughly relevant object lesson on the Cross of Jesus Christ and its effect within and upon society, and that is the focal point of our investigation here. In a small way, we catch the aroma of the Cross, at least the slightest scent of it, through the debate as, once again, the Cross becomes a dividing line.

The Cross divides, it separates and polarizes, extracting and even demanding reactions and responses. The Cross is the symbol of Jesus; it is the work of his earthly life. The Cross was God the Father's conception, and it was his intention before he committed the act of Creation. The Cross is the instrument of redemption, and even redemption itself is a controversy.

The Cross Before Creation

The Cross of Jesus Christ came before Creation. It has always astounded me that God, with his perfect foreknowledge of all things, certainly knew before enacting the Creation that mankind would fall into sin. He knew before the first creative act that we would break his heart; that we would miss the mark, and that we would, if we were to survive, need saving. God knew that he would be the only one who could do it. God knew that if his Creation and its crowning creature, man himself, were to pull through, then in the future his Son must become the Christ, and that the only possible future path for the Christ must be the path to the Cross.

This is what I think of whenever I hear God's pronouncement from the book of Genesis, as he surveyed all that he had created, that it was "very good." It was indeed very good, it was indeed perfect, because it had redemption built into it; the ultimate failsafe mechanism. Creation had, as its finest feature and as its perfect center, the Cross. God could look ahead, even beyond the physical fact of the Cross, and see its healing, saving, sustaining effect. He could see that it was very good.

God could look past the final pronouncement of judgment to be made by the Cross. He could look past the settling of every account for all eternity to be initiated at the Cross and carried out with finality at the judgment throne of God, and he could see that it was, indeed, very, very good. Very good, and yet on the part of man so very hard to accept. The taste of sin's remedy causes many, perhaps even most, to choke. Yet Jesus pulled no punches regarding sin's remedy. He knew what would be its effect.

"Do not suppose that I have come to bring peace to the earth. I did not come to bring peace, but a sword.

For I have come to turn 'a man against his father, a daughter against her mother, a daughter-in-law against her mother-in-law - a man's enemies will be the members of his own household.'"[63]

Stat Crux

"Stat crux dum volvitur orbis"
"The cross remains constant as the world turns"

When *The Passion of the Christ* neared its release, I had quite a struggle regarding how I should respond to it or approach it.

My sentiments cycled from at first believing that this movie would be the single greatest tool for sharing the gospel in the 2,000 years since Jesus walked the earth, to not wanting even to see it, ultimately settling somewhere in between. It is not, of course, the single greatest tool for sharing the gospel. That position still quite safely and exclusively rests with the Word of God and the work of the Holy Spirit. *The Passion of the Christ* is a depiction and a dramatization of a portion of the Word of God, as interpreted by Mel Gibson. It is *not* "the Word" of God.

I weighed a number of arguments and issues and at first decided I didn't want to see the movie. Jim Caviezel is not Jesus Christ, despite the observations that the initials for his name are "JC," and he was thirty-three years old at the making of *The Passion of the Christ.* He is not my Savior, and he did not suffer or die for my sins, even if it is true that he was "struck by lightning" during the filming and that the crucifixion scenes left him physically cold and exhausted.

Human beings are prone to create icons to worship. They love bowing down to that which they can see and touch. The Lord takes great exception to this, which is why he wrote the second commandment:

"You shall not make for yourself an idol in the form of anything in heaven above or on the earth beneath or in the waters below. You shall not bow down to them or worship them; for I, the LORD your God, am a jealous God, punishing the children for the sin of the fathers to the third and fourth generation of those who hate me, but showing love to a thousand generations of those who love me and keep my commandments."[64]

I became concerned that many individuals would idolize Jim Caviezel, and that his image would become that of the Christ to them. For those people, whose minds are pliable and controllable and empty of the true Word of God, Jesus' face would be that of Jim Caviezel. Jesus would move, in their minds, to the haunting, forlorn melodies of John Debney's musical score.

One must conclude that God himself had a significant reason for never allowing a physical description of Christ to be given in his Word. Perhaps it has to do with the transcendence over the physical that the real Christ commands.

I take exception to the references in interviews with Jim and with Mel Gibson relative to Jim's "suffering" as he made the movie. The inference is that he learned something of the suffering of Christ, which he did not. He did not approach the suffering of a true crucifixion, let alone the true Passion of the Christ, and to insinuate that he had any form of involvement with that suffering is erroneous. To go there, then, indicates to me a fundamental flaw in the actor and the writer - co-producer - director's way of thinking.

The focus on the physical suffering of Christ has biblical roots, since the gospels all depict the physical event, but it is misguided in the movie, taking on more the flavor of being the end than the means.

I take exception that *The Passion*, rather than referring to the Pascal sacrifice of our Savior for our sins, now more popularly refers to a Mel Gibson movie and the "sacrifice" of Jim Caviezel on a movie set. "*The Passion of the Christ*? Oh yeah, I saw that. Been there, done that. It was good. But I was a little bit disappointed. I thought Mel was going to be in it." But Mel wasn't in it, you see, nor was Jim Caviezel in any way present at the main event, other than the fact that they, along with you and I, were present in the heart of Christ upon that Cross.

Sensory De-Stimulation

My biggest concern is over the desensitization to the Cross of Christ that now follows the "real to life" cinematic version. At first it cost us ten bucks to "behold the man" on the cross. It cost us a deep emotional investment as we sat in the theaters and heard the whip and the hammer and the groans and the suffering in Surround Sound with a mega-bass boost. We left our popcorn untouched and the fizz softly blurping out of our half-gallon sodas. We didn't even dare go out to the restroom. It just didn't seem right. And we sat, dumbfounded, all the way through the rolling of the credits, silent, until the lights finally came up. The first time, anyway.

Then we could behold him for a buck and a half, and it was a little less costly in every other way as well. And after we've viewed our DVD version (smaller and less engulfing, certainly) enough times that our per-episode investment is only two bits or so, we will have assimilated the whole concept, and will have put it on the same shelf in our minds as the disemboweling in Braveheat or the baby extra-terrestrial monster ripping itself out of that guy's stomach in Alien.

See how compelling even the depiction, the dramatization, of Christ's Cross can be?

All of these issues concern me deeply, but upon their thorough consideration, and after observing some of the initial response to the film, my position began to soften a bit. I began to realize that the cross, the real Cross of Calvary, is bigger than all of that. The Cross is bigger than Jim Caviezel. The Cross transcends Hollywood. It transcends demented ideas, and even the crass marketing machines that would merchandise its nails and would profit from it. It transcends culture, past and present . . . in fact, the Cross creates its own culture, unique from any other at any time in any place. And we have been trivializing the Cross for many hundreds of years, desensitizing ourselves to its message regardless of the medium by which it has been delivered. Our Bibles have hibernated, covers dusty and unworn, for years at a time; the world's least read, least understood, most discussed, most ignored, most misquoted, most misinterpreted bestseller.

The Cultural Irrelevancy of the Cross

For a while I thought that I didn't want to sacrifice myself at the altar of cultural relevancy for the sake of watching a magnified Passion play. Besides, there is nothing culturally relevant about the Cross in the minds of our modern world. Today, across the broadest spectrum of American society, and even around the world, we just don't get it. There is a very low level of comprehension regarding the true nature of the Cross.

But then I realized that this is *my* culture. I own it as much as the next person, and I am as responsible for its existence in its present form as anyone. And from this movie there arose some thoughtful consideration of the issues surrounding and comprising the Cross. In that I found the redemptive element.

The Cross is bigger than all the hype and all the misconception combined. It is bigger than a wrong-headed but good-hearted emphasis, and it is bigger than spin masters and profit machines. In a certain sense, it is almost appropriate that market-driven people with a marketing mindset have raised the Cross in the marketplace. It can speak its diametric opposition to such an environment most powerfully as it is planted in its midst. Please understand that this statement comes from one who most vigorously affirms our system of free enterprise, and has nothing against marketing at all. It is just that I abhor the marketing of the Cross.

We all heard and read the many debates on this blockbuster movie. They came from every quarter. I read noted film critic Roger Ebert's review in shock. It was a theologically oriented consideration that I never would have expected out of the entertainment industry, under the headline, *"The Passion" uncompromising*. Please bear with a somewhat lengthy quote, which I feel is worth every word to make an important point.

Roger Ebert: Theologian

"What Gibson has provided for me, for the first time in my life, is a visceral idea of what the Passion consisted of. That his film is superficial in terms of the surrounding message - that we get only a few passing references to the teachings of Jesus - is, I suppose, not the point. This is not a sermon or a homily, but a visualization of the central event in the Christian religion. Take it or leave it.

"David Ansen, a critic I respect, finds in Newsweek that Gibson has gone too far. ". . . (T)he relentless gore is self-defeating," he writes. "Instead of being moved by Christ's suffering, or awed by his sacrifice, I felt abused by a filmmaker intent on punishing an audience, for who knows what sins." This is a completely valid response to the film, and I quote Ansen because I suspect he speaks for many audience members, who will enter the theater in a devout or spiritual mood and emerge deeply disturbed. You must be prepared for whipping, flayings, beatings, the crunch of bones, the agony of screams, the cruelty of the sadistic centurions, the rivulets of blood that crisscross every inch of Jesus' body. Some will leave before the end.

"This is not a Passion like any other ever filmed. Perhaps that is the best reason for it. I grew up on those pious Hollywood biblical epics of the 1950s, which looked like holy cards brought to life. I remember my grin when Time magazine noted that Jeffrey Hunter, starring as Christ in "King of Kings" (1961), had shaved his armpits. (Not Hunter's fault; the film's crucifixion scene had to be reshot because preview audiences objected to Jesus' hairy chest.) If it does nothing else, Gibson's film will break the tradition of turning Jesus and his disciples into neat, clean, well-barbered middle-class businessmen. They were poor men in a poor land. I debated Scorsese's "The Last Temptation of Christ" with Michael Medved before an audience from a Christian college, and was told by an audience member that the characters were filthy and needed haircuts.

"The Middle East in biblical times was a Jewish community occupied against its will by the Roman Empire, and the message of Jesus was equally threatening to both sides - to the Romans, because he was a revolutionary, and to the establishment of Jewish priests because he preached a new covenant and threatened the status quo. In the movie's scenes showing Jesus being condemned to death, the two

Jim Otis

main players are Pontius Pilate, the Roman governor, and Caiaphas, the Jewish high priest. Both men want to keep the lid on, and while neither is especially eager to see Jesus crucified, they live in a harsh time when such a man is dangerous.

"Pilate is seen going through his well-known doubts before finally washing his hands of the matter and turning Jesus over to the priests, but Caiaphas, who also had doubts, is not seen as sympathetically. The critic Steven D. Greydanus, in a useful analysis of the film, writes: "The film omits the canonical line from John's gospel in which Caiaphas argues that it is better for one man to die for the people that the nation be saved. Had Gibson retained this line, perhaps giving Caiaphas a measure of the inner conflict he gave to Pilate, it could have underscored the similarities between Caiaphas and Pilate and helped defuse the issue of anti-Semitism."

"This scene and others might justifiably be cited by anyone concerned that the movie contains anti-Semitism. My own feeling is that Gibson's film is not anti-Semitic, but reflects a range of behavior on the part of its Jewish characters, on balance favorably. The Jews who seem to desire Jesus' death are in the priesthood, and have political as well as theological reasons for acting; like today's Catholic bishops who were slow to condemn abusive priests, Protestant TV preachers, who confuse religion with politics, or Muslim clerics who are silent on terrorism, they have an investment in their positions and authority. The other Jews seen in the film are viewed positively;

Simon helps Jesus to carry the cross, Veronica brings a cloth to wipe his face, Jews in the crowd cry out against his torture.

"A reasonable person, I believe, will reflect that in this story set in a Jewish land, there are many characters with many motives, some good, some not, each one representing himself, none representing his religion. The story involves a Jew who tried no less than to replace the established religion and set himself up as the Messiah. He was understandably greeted with a jaundiced eye by the Jewish establishment while at the same time finding his support, his disciples, and the founders of his church entirely among his fellow Jews. The libel that the Jews "killed Christ" involves a willful misreading of testament and teaching: Jesus was made man and came to Earth IN ORDER to suffer and die in reparation for our sins. No race, no religion, no man, no priest, no governor, no executioner killed Jesus; he died by God's will to fulfill his purpose, and with our sins we ALL killed him. That some Christian churches have historically been guilty of the sin of anti-Semitism is undeniable, but in committing it they violated their own beliefs.

"This discussion will seem beside the point for readers who want to know about the movie, not the theology. But "The Passion of the Christ," more than any other film I can recall, depends upon theological considerations. Gibson has not made a movie that anyone would call "commercial," and if it grosses millions, that will not be because anyone was entertained. It is a personal message movie of the most radical kind, attempting to re-create events of personal urgency to Gibson. The filmmaker has put his artistry and fortune at the service of his conviction and belief, and that doesn't happen often.

Is the film "good" or "great?" I imagine each person's reaction (visceral, theological, artistic) will differ. I was moved by the depth of feeling, by the skill of the actors and technicians, by their desire to see this project through, no matter what. To discuss individual performances, such as James Caviezel's heroic depiction of the ordeal, is almost beside the point. This isn't a movie about performances, although it has powerful ones; or about technique, although it is awesome; or about cinematography (although Caleb Deschanel paints with an artist's eye); or music (although John Debney supports the content without distracting from it). It is a film about an idea. An idea that it is necessary to fully comprehend the Passion if Christianity is to make any sense. Gibson has communicated his idea with a single-minded urgency. Many will disagree. Some will agree, but be horrified by the graphic treatment. I myself am no longer religious in the sense that a long-ago altar boy thought he should be; but I can respond to the power of belief whether I agree or not, and when I find it in a film I must respect it."[65]

There's the Crux

Roger Ebert's analysis took me over the edge. These are exactly the topics of conversation and debate that I long to embrace with the pre-Christian or the nominal or even lapsed Christian. I decided I would see the film because I wanted to be able to address the issues it raises, even if those issues would only be at the forefront of America's thinking for the proverbial "fifteen minutes." They would be fifteen precious minutes.

The Cross was, at least momentarily, again at the crux of society. It was the crossroads, the fork, the point where one road becomes two, just as it is in your own life. The Cross became once again the enigma that puzzled us, the unsolvable riddle, the pivotal point, and the apex. The Cross became crucial, a direction that could be taken and a signpost pointing the way. The Cross became an issue of debate and the grounds and the occasion for making either a deliberate choice or a flat refusal. The Cross was once again, as always, the Crux, fulfilling its centuries-old role; no, more than that, it was fulfilling its *eternal* role.

Chapter Fifteen
Skandalon!

The Cross is Heaven's eternal offense to millions. The Greek word depicting the offense of the Cross pokes at the very core of its essence. It is the word "*skandalon*," from which we derive, as you might guess, the word scandal, and also from which is derived the term "stumbling block." The Bible freely calls Christ and his Cross an offense and a stumbling block, both prophetically and historically. You can begin to get the sense of it as you read some of the various references.

"but we preach Christ crucified: a stumbling block to Jews and foolishness to Gentiles"[66]

"Why not?" [Why did Israel not obtain righteousness?] *"Because they pursued it not by faith but as if it were by works. They stumbled over the 'stumbling stone.' As it is written: 'See, I lay in Zion a stone that causes men to stumble and a rock that makes them fall, and the one who trusts in him will never be put to shame.'"*[67]

"The LORD Almighty is the one you are to regard as holy, he is the one you are to fear, he is the one you are to dread, and he will be a sanctuary; but for both houses of Israel he will be a stone that causes men to stumble and a rock that makes them fall. And for the people of Jerusalem he will be a trap and a

snare. Many of them will stumble; they will fall and be broken, they will be snared and captured."[68]

"As you come to him, the living Stone - rejected by men but chosen by God and precious to him - you also, like living stones, are being built into a spiritual house to be a holy priesthood, offering spiritual sacrifices acceptable to God through Jesus Christ. For in Scripture it says: 'See, I lay a stone in Zion, a chosen and precious cornerstone, and the one who trusts in him will never be put to shame.'

Now to you who believe, this stone is precious. But to those who do not believe, 'The stone the builders rejected has become the capstone,' and, 'A stone that causes men to stumble and a rock that makes them fall.' They stumble because they disobey the message - which is also what they were destined for."[69]

*"Who has believed our message
and to whom has the arm of the LORD been revealed?
He grew up before him like a tender shoot,
and like a root out of dry ground.
He had no beauty or majesty to attract us to him,*

*nothing in his appearance that we should desire
him.
He was despised and rejected by men,
a man of sorrows, and familiar with suffering.
Like one from whom men hide their faces
he was despised, and we esteemed him not.
Surely he took up our infirmities
and carried our sorrows,*

yet we considered him stricken by God,
smitten by him, and afflicted.
But he was pierced for our transgressions,
he was crushed for our iniquities;
the punishment that brought us peace was upon him,
and by his wounds we are healed.
We all, like sheep, have gone astray,
each of us has turned to his own way;
and the LORD has laid on him
the iniquity of us all.
He was oppressed and afflicted,
yet he did not open his mouth;
he was led like a lamb to the slaughter,
and as a sheep before her shearers is silent,
so he did not open his mouth.
By oppression and judgment he was taken away.
And who can speak of his descendants?
For he was cut off from the land of the living;
for the transgression of my people he was stricken.
He was assigned a grave with the wicked,
and with the rich in his death,
though he had done no violence,
nor was any deceit in his mouth.
Yet it was the LORD's will to crush him and cause

him to suffer,
and though the LORD makes his life a guilt offering,
he will see his offspring and prolong his days,
and the will of the LORD will prosper in his hand.
After the suffering of his soul,
he will see the light of life and be satisfied;

by his knowledge my righteous servant will justify
many,
and he will bear their iniquities.
Therefore I will give him a portion among the great,
and he will divide the spoils with the strong,
because he poured out his life unto death,
and was numbered with the transgressors.
For he bore the sin of many,
and made intercession for the transgressors. "[70]

The Trigger in the Trap

The word *skandalon* speaks to the offensive nature of the Cross, and to all the inferences that come out of it. "*Skandalon* denotes 'the trigger in the trap' on which the bait is placed, and which, when touched by the animal, springs and causes it to close causing entrapment. The word and its derivatives belong only to biblical and ecclesiastical Greek.

"*Skandalon* always denotes the enticement or the occasion that leads to ruin and rarely denotes merely a hidden, unexpected cause of ruin."[71]

How, then, do we apply this to the Cross? Besides the brutality of it all, to which we take such great exception and by which we all *are* so offended, what about it repulses us, and what of its essence entraps us?

The Triple Whammy

It is simply this: We are offended at the thought that such violence, such merciless punishment, was both deserved by us yet meted out to one who took it in our place. In my place. In *your* place. Three aspects of this deep offense come to mind, constituting a triply offensive whammy.

Whammy One: Why the Big Show?

First is the idea that God, or anyone for that matter, should require the Cross. Why, after all, could sin not simply be forgiven? Why would God have to make such a big show of it? Why the horror and the drama and even the melodrama of the Cross? Why did Jesus have to die, and worse, why did his dying necessitate such agony? The forthright explanation that sin is so serious and killing in its own right that it deserves such punishment; that God is so righteous and just that he must demand such punishment; and that we are unworthy to effect anything beyond our own dying should we undergo such punishment never seems to be enough. We do not think like God, nor are we prone to accept his charity.

There is something about the public proclamation of the Cross that damns us in and of itself. It holds our sin and our inadequacy up to public knowledge, scrutiny and ridicule. It somehow seems that if God had a sense of good taste and a bit more discretion he would transact this business quietly. In this publicizing of the whole affair, we are stripped of all dignity. Or are we?

Whammy Two: I Don't Deserve This!

Second is the insinuation, or rather the proclamation, that we are considered to be deserving of our own cross. If we are to benefit from this sacrifice, in fact, we must *consider ourselves* to deserve that very same punishment. I bridle against that, but I must accept it, even confess it, and so must you.

Part of the process, and a critical element of salvation itself, is the aspect of confession that indicates not only that I admit my sin, but also that I confess or say the same thing about it that God says. Namely, sin is so vile and so hurting in and of itself, it so mars and defaces the perfect creation of God, it so flies in the face of God's holiness, it so debases my interaction with my fellow man that because I have so personally embraced and perpetuated it *I now, by virtue of my participation in sin, deserve the Cross.* I deserve the wages of sin, which is death. I fully deserve this eternal, public consequence.

The Final Whammy: I Bring Nothing to This Table

Third is the insinuation that I myself am considered unworthy even to bear this Cross. I cannot even carry it, let alone endure it with any effect. I cannot do it on my own behalf, or on that of anyone else. My tendency, particularly as an independent, free, entrepreneurial American, is to "pay my own way." If I sense the gravity of my sin, my inclination is to want to make it right. If there's any restitution to be made, any redemption to be bartered, I'll be doing all of that on my own behalf, thank you very much.

But I cannot make this restitution. I cannot pay this price, and it offends me. It's like walking into a town and being told my money isn't wanted there, that the currency I bear is worthless. It's as if there is a sign at the foot of this Cross, stating, "Your payment is no good here." So even if I want to pay, I cannot. I am not worthy to pay this price. The lucre of my life is no good. I have nothing of value to bring to this transaction. Not even, to state it pointedly, my skills of negotiation.

Only His Cross Will Do

If there is to be any salvation at all the Cross, his Cross, is required, but I have no part in it other than receiving its benefit. That leaves me a beggar. *Skandalon,* indeed. That trips my trigger; the trigger of my pride, the trigger of my rebellion, the trigger of my "dignity." But none of those responses moves God. The Cross *remains* . . . as my world turns. I have either to deny it or to embrace it. *There* is the crux of my life, *and of yours.*

Chapter Sixteen
Counter-Vortex

My Sam's

Sometimes our Friday nights are the absolute apex of our week, or at least of mine, if not my wife's, even though there is nothing glamorous about them. It's just that we usually have Friday nights as our private, personal time. We will go shopping and grab a meal out at a restaurant, sometimes at a nice place and sometimes nothing fancy, but we love it. I particularly love to go to Grape Road, which is where our major shopping opportunities all converge. It's a forty-minute drive, but it is *so* worth it! We've got Barnes and Noble there, along with Outback, Meijer, Bed, Bath and Beyond, a huge Best Buy, the University Park Mall and zillions of other stores and restaurants.

Most importantly, though, we've got Sam's up there on Grape Road, or just off of it. Not just any Sam's (we irreverently leave off the "Club" part, even though it upsets them when we try to write a check that way), but it's a Super Sam's. It's the big one. Oh yeah, it's a biggie. I can get lost in that place. We really don't overspend our budget at Sam's any more. I'm proud that it only took us about twenty years to master that part of it. We've finally learned our limits, and we shop for great deals on stuff we really need. Occasionally, I discover something there that I didn't realize I needed. In fact, I may not have realized it even existed before I saw it there, but I really, really need it when I discover it. So it's a good thing that

141

Sam's is there, educating me, even saving me from my own ignorance.

Accommodate Me!

I offer all of that for no particular reason except to say that I was educated at Sam's recently in a different way than that. It was one of our golden Friday nights and I was wandering the aisles when I was nearly run over. The culprit was a lady; a very, very large lady, driving one of those electric carts. She was weaving and dodging all around, going too fast, impatiently zipping up behind and nearly crushing the heels of every mere pedestrian who inadvertently got in her way. It was quite a procession, since she had taken a regular shopping cart and was pushing that along as well, and none too skillfully. She was handicapped, but the biggest handicap was not the physical one, it was the stunting and the hardening of her attitude.

As she wound her way briskly through the sacred streets of my Sam's it was all too obvious that she felt a high degree of entitlement. She was mad at those of us who were walking. She was mad that we didn't honor her handicap quite as quickly and seriously as she thought we should. She was impatient that we who were ambulating our way through life were doing it at a far slower pace than she was able to achieve with those electric wheels propelling her astonishing girth. I worried a bit about the whole idea of momentum.

I admit it. I looked at the stuff she was cramming in her cart, and it wasn't healthy. In fact, it was gross. Grossly non-nutritious and grossly fattening food. Rich deserts, fried foods, fatty, oily snacks, and nothing but. It wasn't my business, but having just watched a documentary that identified America's leading new handicap as morbid obesity, I wondered if that was her circumstance. I was certain she was handicapped by true physical ailments, but I couldn't help wondering if those ailments were not magnified by what literally had to be a couple hundred pounds of excess fat. When she had brusquely breezed by, I tried to forget it. It wasn't my problem.

Attitudes on Parade

Later, at the checkout, I heard a huge commotion a couple aisles over. You guessed it; she was back, only times two. Her cart and electric buggy menagerie had turned into a virtual circus train because an equally handicapped daughter had joined her. The physical resemblance was undeniable, right down to the issue of their weight and their identical attitudes. The daughter had her own buggy and cart combination, and the two of them were rudely inching up on an elderly couple in front of them, obviously peeved that the sea of customers had not parted to allow them a privileged passage to the front of the line. They waited with pained impatience, carts loaded to the groaning point. There was a great deal of sighing and huffing, but I was a little surprised when I realized it was coming from me.

The point is that these women had an expectation, reinforced and even encouraged by our society. They knew they were entitled. Their behavior made it obvious that they believed their environment owed them something, and therefore had the obligation to accommodate them. The store had an obligation to provide them a special and expensive means of conveyance. The other shoppers had an obligation to yield to them, and to anticipate their needs, surrendering their own position or rights in deference to the handicapped status of these women, to the point where, even though they were sitting while others stood, they should not have been expected to sit in line. Their entitlement was not just to equality, but also to superiority, to a unique and "special" go-to-the-head-of-the-class status that superseded the boundaries of common courtesy, human cooperation and even simple pleasant civility.

I'm not trying to deride or disrespect these women, but rather to make the point that there is a certain amount of that same attitude infecting each of us.

Scrap the Standard

I recently read an Associated Press report from Nashville, Tennessee, announcing that student honor rolls in that city have come under fire, "[a]fter a few parents complained that their children might be ridiculed for not making the list, . . ." The schools all stopped posting honor rolls, as some considered banning the hanging of good work in the hallways – "all at the advice of school lawyers." Apparently, the underachievers were embarrassed. As the typical over-reactionary result, "[s]ome schools have since put a stop to academic pep rallies. Others think they may have to cancel spelling bees." "[Other schools] think it might be a good idea to get rid of the honor roll altogether," as one principal did in Nashville. "The rationale was, if there are some children that always make it and others that always don't make it, there is a very subtle message that was sent," he said. "I also understand right to privacy is the legal issue for the new century.

"I discourage competitive games at school," he said. "They just don't fit my worldview of what a school should be."[72]

O You Dog-Wagging Tail . . .

In a Los Angeles Times editorial by Margaret A. Hagen, she describes the Equal Employment Opportunity Commission's new guidelines forbidding employment discrimination and mandating employer accommodation of mental disabilities. The American Psychiatric Association's diagnostic manual lists 374 mental disorders that are potentially deserving of accommodation by employers under the Americans With Disabilities Act of 1990.

The depressive who is groggy in the morning from medication is not asked to rise earlier in order to be fully awake for the job because the EEOC has specified that it is the employer who is required to accommodate the sleepiness.

Even where the disabled worker suffers from "intermittent explosive disorder" - repeated "episodes of failure to resist aggressive impulses that result in serious acts or destruction of property" - the workplace must accommodate him.

But the category of disorder that most boggles the mind as necessitating employer accommodation rather than employee behavioral adjustment is that of the personality [misalignment called] "antisocial personality disorder." Persons with this affliction used to be known as *sociopaths*.

According to the psychiatric diagnostic manual, this distressing disorder is characterized by "repeatedly performing acts that are grounds for arrest . . . repeated lying, use of aliases or conning others for personal profit or pleasure . . . irritability and aggressiveness, as indicated by repeated physical fights or assaults, reckless disregard for safety of self or others, consistent irresponsibility, as indicated by repeated failure to sustain consistent work behavior or honor financial obligations."[73]

Doing the Party-Boat Flip

I heard my wife snickering as she took in the morning news. The item that tickled her was about a party-boat in Texas:

AUSTIN, Texas - Partygoers apparently hoping to catch a glimpse of nude sunbathers crowded on one side of a floating barge, prompting the ship to capsize and dump all 60 people into Lake Travis.

Two people were hospitalized with minor injuries Sunday after the rented double-decker barge sank near Hippie Hollow, a lakeside park and the only public nude beach in Texas.

The accident occurred during Splash Day, a semiannual event hosted at the clothing-optional area by the Austin Tavern Guild, a gay and lesbian bar association.

Witnesses said that all of the people aboard the barge moved to one side as it neared Hippie Hollow, creating uneven distribution and making it tilt. It sank in 50-foot-deep water.

Krista Umscheid, a spokeswoman for the Lower Colorado River Authority, said that although everyone aboard was accounted for, Travis County sheriff's divers were checking compartments of the sunken pontoon boat as a precaution.[74]

Where's the Parallel?

This is it. This is where we've gone with sin. When we're handicapped with it, we get a case of the attitude, and we're all too willing to take it on parade. We see our sin as a handicap, and we believe that it should, it *must*, be accommodated. Get out of my way! Attitude coming through! Handicap in the store! Make way! When confronted by its excess, we crowd to the side of the barge until we capsize.

When a comparative standard of performance embarrasses us, there's a simple solution: Eliminate the standard. Better yet, *make the standard the culprit.* Make it the evil. Make underachievement the new

147

healthy standard. Celebrate underachievement and mediocrity!

When our behavior is caustic, destructive, selfish and counter-productive, foist it onto others anyway. Force them to accept it. Test their tolerance! Damn them if they don't pass our test! And, of course, damn them if they damn us for doing our damning.

But Let's Check the Bottom Line

Yet we must, to be fair, look at our society. Has the new tolerance made us better, or merely discourteous and self-involved? Has the lowering of our standards made us more competitive, or just a bigger bunch of better losers? Has our surrender to the ridiculous made us more effective, or simply slaves of the nonsensical? Has our constant gazing at the excess of sin in our society made us feel more fulfilled, or just caused us to topple into the drink?

I propose it has accomplished the latter in each case, as does our acquiescence to our personal sin. And that runs contrary to the image in which we were created, and which we are constructed to emulate. Although we are decidedly sinful by nature, we are drawn to God by powerful cords, thus causing our participation in sin to run contrary to our intended spiritual disposition. So, we experience an uncomfortable, emptying dissonance of our natures.

If we are ever to experience salvation from sin, we must recognize that we don't need to learn to better accommodate our sin, but instead *we need a Savior*. We don't need a lower standard; we need a Redeemer.

We don't need to inflict our miserable dysfunction on everyone else; we need a Re-Creator, a Deliverer.

The Apostle Paul wrote of certain critics:

We do not dare to classify or compare ourselves with some who commend themselves. When they measure themselves by themselves and compare themselves with themselves, they are not wise.[75]

Oh, Lord, make us wise.

The Substance of Grace

It takes something very special to wipe out my sin and to knock out this dissonance of natures warring within me, and that special thing is grace. Grace has been made into an acronym, at times said to mean "God's Riches At Christ's Expense." In other words, it is in a sense the driving dynamic behind the very thing that saves me, and is provided completely and exclusively by God, with nothing of myself adding to or subtracting from it. This grace is a perfect, free and complete thing in itself. The following illustration may help us understand it. I don't know if this story is true or not, but it certainly is illustrative.

A Class on Grace

I left work early so I could have some uninterrupted study time right before the final in my Youth Issues class. When I got to class, everybody was doing their last minute studying.

The teacher came in and said he would review with us for just a little bit before the test. We went through the review, most of it right on the study guide, but there were some things he was reviewing with which I was unfamiliar. When questioned about it, he said that they were in the book and we were responsible for everything in the book. We couldn't really argue with that.

Finally it was time to take the test.

"Leave them face down on the desk until everyone has one, and I'll tell you when to start," our professor instructed.

When we turned them over, every answer on the test was filled in! The bottom of the last page said the following:

"This is the end of the Final Exam. All the answers on your test are correct. You will receive an 'A' on the final exam. The reason you passed the test is because the creator of the test took it for you. All the work you did in preparation for this test did not help you get the A. You have just experienced GRACE."

He then went around the room and asked each student individually: "What is your grade? Do you deserve the grade you are receiving? How much did all your studying for this exam help you achieve your final grade?"

Now I am not a crier by any stretch of the imagination, but I had to fight back tears when answering those questions and thinking about how the Creator has passed the test for me.

Discussion afterward went like this: "I have tried to teach you all semester that you are a recipient of grace. I've tried to communicate to you that you need to demonstrate this gift as you work with young people. Don't hammer them; they are not the enemy. Help them, for they will carry on your ministry if it is full of GRACE!"

Talking about how some of us had probably studied hours and some just a few minutes but had all received the same grade, he pointed to a story Jesus told in Matthew 20. The owner of a vineyard hired people to work in his field and agreed to pay them a certain amount. Several different times during the day, he hired more workers. When it was time to pay them, they all received the same amount. When the ones who had been hired first thing in the morning began complaining, the boss said, "Should you be angry because I am kind?" (Matthew 20:15).

The teacher said he had never provided this kind of final examination before and probably would never do it again, but because of the content of many of our class discussions, he felt like we needed to experience grace.

The Vortex of Amazing Grace

I've never experienced a serendipity as unlikely as that final exam must have been for a number of those students. In fact, it's so unusual that the story smacks of urban legend to me. But we live on the edge of such grace when it comes to our relationship with the living God. As much as we may be caught in the Terminal Vortex of Sin, yet we are within a hair's breadth of the trap, the *skandalon* God has set to defeat it. We are just a realization and a breath away from God's superior Vortex of Amazing Grace.

Are you swirling about in the Terminal Vortex, swamped and mired in the muck that is the unavoidable byproduct of plain spiritual lostness? It can take many different forms, yet each form is so predictable and so intertwined with all the others. Perhaps you are drowning in the residual bitterness and rejection of a marriage gone bad or a painful divorce.

Or you may be the victim of the horrendous, capricious circumstances of every day living, and instead of finding the daily rat-race fulfilling or rewarding, you're running on spiritual empty, with no joy, no peace, and a foreboding sense that after everything is said and done something, no . . . *everything*, is missing. You're coming up short.

Maybe you're dealing with confusion, or addiction, depression or the sense of futility and helplessness that comes with chronic or even terminal illness and pain. Perhaps you're experiencing the sense of dread and desperation that comes with terrible guilt, and try as you might you have never been able to discover relief, and there is no place in which you can find release. Perhaps you've just settled into a privileged life of leisure, but you're coming to the haunting realization that you do not do anything, nor have you achieved anything, of lasting significance, so you feel your life is meaningless and petty.

Or you might be plagued with a sense of unrealistic expectations; perfectionism and its cousin procrastination may rule your life, born out of a history of family dysfunction or disconnectedness. You may even be one of the millions today who has been sucked up into the relentless vacuum of empty religion, working hard and harder to meet the impossible standards of some inscrutable, unyielding, graceless god.

Whatever your case may be, the real God's genuine grace is but a choice away. You're nearly there, you're on the very edge of it; you're being tugged into the outer ripples of God's Vortex of Amazing Grace, as have been so many, many others before you. Just move a little closer and he'll pull you in, and once you've entered you will experience forgiveness, release, wholeness, healing, renewal, re-creation, and all the wonderment of God's engulfing, cleansing, strengthening love. You'll be set right and sustained. Amazing, yes. Truly Amazing.

The Grace that Goes Before Us

You have lived your entire life encompassed by God's grace. Grace surrounds you, grace engulfs you, and grace is the substance of your every breath; it is by grace that you will draw the next. In theological terms, it is called prevenient grace, which means the grace that precedes or the grace that goes before. It is the grace that paves the way to salvation. It is an inviting path, though straight and narrow, and one upon which we all must tread if we are to know God. It is the path that leads us to Salvation.

It is this grace that goes before us that renders moot the argument that God doesn't care about us as individuals, or that God has unfairly neglected to make ample provision for our salvation, we being the infected sin-carriers that we are. Quite the contrary, we are steeped in grace.

God's grace cries out to us from every fiber of the fabric of Creation, "God is! God is here! God has made this, and he has made you!" God's grace cries out to us from within, as the seed of eternal longing he has set in every human heart strives to break its shell, extend its root, pushing into the rocky soil of our spiritual resistance.

God's grace urges you onward through the ministry of the Church, now become God's representation of the living, breathing Body of the resurrected Christ. In a thousand ways the Church confronts you, calls you, beckons you, compels you to come Home.

History, laden with the facts of Christ's life, death and resurrection and countless stories of man's failure and need, deals God's grace to you with every lesson. Archaeology proves history, including biblical history, and from it God's truth and grace are proclaimed. Legions upon legions of God-seekers, turned into God-finders, who both exist today and who have gone before, are stamped with the grace of God and their testimonies serve as the clarion rally-cry, sounding again and again, "Grace! Grace to you from the all knowing, all sufficient, all wonderful, loving God! Grace, wrapped in mercy, presented by none less than the Person of the Living Christ, direct from God's heart to you!"

Grace goes before you, grace pours out upon you. Grace is beside you, underneath you, all around you. Grace has your back. Grace paves your way. Grace directs you, grace abounds. Oh, that the wondrous grace of God would overwhelm you.

Your Choice

Luke 19:41-46 NIV

As he approached Jerusalem and saw the city, he wept over it and said, "If you, even you, had only known on this day what would bring you peace-but now it is hidden from your eyes. The days will come upon you when your enemies will build an embankment against you and encircle you and hem you in on every side. They will dash you to the ground, you and the children within your walls. They will not leave one stone on another, because you did not recognize the time of God's coming to you."

Then he entered the temple area and began driving out those who were selling. "It is written," he said to them, " 'My house will be a house of prayer'; but you have made it 'a den of robbers.'"

Everything does weigh out in the end, you know. There is justice for evil; there is consequence for both action and neglect. In the end, responsibility is borne by each of us for the stewardship of our opportunities and our choices. In the end, there is reward for the choosing of God's righteousness, and there is retribution for being content in wickedness. In the end, good overcomes evil, Heaven becomes the home of those who chose God's way of grace, and Hell becomes the habitat of those who repeatedly denied it.

We want this ultimate weighing out, because we carry the innate understanding that it is right. It is the only right way. We desire justice. We don't want a pass on this, even for ourselves, because we know it would make eternity an unworthy place and an unworthy concept. No, we want God to be God, and we want him to hold to it.

With this desire, we understand that we cannot earn our way into righteousness, but that a way has been provided on our behalf. That's wondrous to us too, because it means the loser can win and the underdog can come out on top. It means the humble hometown boy and girl can make good. It means that the one who never had a chance finds one anyway. It means the hopeless team can make an unbelievable comeback, and after all, we all love a great comeback story, don't we? It means we all can choose, we all can score, we all are free and all accounts will be settled when everything is said and done. Eternity has a bottom line after all, and we can depend on it. There is truth, there is justice, and there are some things that will never, ever change. Though everything around us is prone to disappoint us, though we disappoint one another and especially ourselves, there is one thing that holds true: The Cross remains as the world turns, and so it will remain forever.

God insists, given the pool of prevenient grace in which we are swimming, that we must choose. He weeps when we stubbornly reject him, loving our sin more than his holiness and the wonder of actually knowing God himself, yet, even though it is done through his tears, his temple will be cleansed and all will be set right. God weeps when we refuse to recognize the moment of his arrival, the day of his coming, the time of our visitation. He weeps because he knows the wages of sin, and he knows the price he has paid.

No Gimmicks, No Tricks

Whenever I get a special offer, particularly by email, I doubt it. There is, invariably, a catch. Just today I was told that I could sit in my living room in boxer shorts and my bathrobe and answer surveys online, earning literally thousands of dollars every month. They said they needed me to do this, that the opportunities to do this were overwhelming, and they begged me to participate. The fine print, of course, was that I had to buy in. It was a sure thing, but they could offer *no guarantees.* It was worth oh-so-much-more than the paltry sum they were almost embarrassed to ask me to pay, but they couldn't be sure that I would make that paltry sum back, let alone more. I probably get a hundred offers like that every year, just as you do, and my skept-o-meter goes off the charts with each one.

Human offers are tricky and always have a hidden clause. God offers you pure grace, however; a prepaid entrance into eternal life. You are free to choose, and once you do you will receive all of the features and benefits that come from living in God's Kingdom:

- You become a son or daughter of the Living God;

- You receive forgiveness and cleansing for your sins;
- God purposely forgets your past, and his focus is only on the relationship you enjoy with him today and for eternity. When God looks at you he sees not your failure, but the perfect sufficiency of the righteousness of Jesus Christ;
- You literally gain access to God's throne of grace, with free entry into his throne room because of your special family status;
- While you do not become exempt from the challenges, temptations, trials and even the pain of life, you are given the unique strength to persevere, to persist, and not just to endure but to conquer, and with it you receive the deepest, truest sense of eternal "joy unspeakable and full of glory;"
- You are given the right to win, the right to be a forever-overcomer, and the right not only to live in God's victorious Kingdom today, but to enter Heaven at the end of your physical life and to abide there for all eternity.

Before you choose, or before you refuse this offer of grace, I hope you will take a few moments to read the next chapter and catch the scent of grace, the thrill of restoration and the power of re-creation in the life of one human being.

Chapter Seventeen
Dead Man Toucher

Simon

His name was Simon. Once it had been just Simon, but now it was Simon the Leper. He wondered if anyone remembered that he had a name, or if anyone remembered that once he had been a rising star, a successful young entrepreneur. That was before this disease, and the Law, had made him unclean. The Law said, "As long as he has the infection he remains unclean. He must live alone; he must live outside the camp."

"As long as he has the infection?" He would never be free of it. Nobody ever was freed from this type of leprosy, and Simon had it bad. He was one of those unfortunate victims who were known as being full of leprosy.

In the beginning he felt the unaccountable lethargy and pain in his joints. Then the first of the discolored patches had appeared on his skin. Gradually, but soon enough, there followed the open sores, oozing disgustingly. As the disease had its way Simon's whole appearance was hideously transformed. He lost his eyebrows and eyelashes. His eyes took on a strange, dead stare. He became hoarse, his breath coming in thin, wheezing gasps because of the ulceration of his vocal chords. His hands and feet broke out in lesions. Ultimately, he was covered with ugly growths, becoming completely repulsive, both to himself and others.

Simon lost sensation slowly, sometimes even surprisingly. The day came when he scalded himself terribly in a fire, but felt no pain whatsoever. His fingers, his toes, eventually even his nose and his ears decayed and fell off.

The Living Dead

Simon the Leper was dead. He was a living, progressively decaying physically dead man, but he was dead in so many other ways, too. He was dead socially, spiritually and economically. He had no friends but other lepers in the caves. He couldn't go to Temple any more. Even the priests disdained him. There were no merciful visitations in the leper camp. At least in later years they would first pronounce the ritual of the dead over the leper before banishing him, but not even that during Simon's lifetime. There was nothing to do but beg for scraps, from a distance, of course. Mostly he relied on the generosity of the less deformed and more successful beggars.

Simon was despised and he was certainly rejected. He was deprived of everything normal, living human beings might hold dear. He would never touch his wife again. He would never know the comfort of her embrace. He would never again toss his little daughter in the air, never again play rough house with his son, never even touch them.

When Simon had been pronounced leprous he had gone directly to the leper caves, and his family knew nothing of him. It was better for them this way. He had gotten word secretly to his wife, but he felt it was better that the children have no father at all than to be known as the children of Simon the Leper. This was the real doom brought upon him by this creeping, killing, infectious curse. Death he could stand, but not this. It was terrible, terrifying, torturous, traumatic, but none too soon terminal, tough terminal it would be. There was simply no way out.

Several years had passed, and his days were worse than Simon could ever have imagined. He was weak, his flesh and his muscles now eaten away. His body was now mostly ulcerated. In the few areas where he could still feel, he had searing, fiery pain. He had lost his appendages. Simon had a total of only five fingers now between both hands, and only three toes on his feet. Walking had become an all-consuming chore, but it didn't matter much because where would he walk, anyway? He'd been reduced to lying about, subsisting on the occasional piece of garbage, waiting and hoping, sometimes begging to die. That was all of hope that he had left; the only hope.

Let's allow Simon to fade to black. I don't know that there's anything we can do for him anyway.

Jesus

Jesus had been working very hard. It was nice being in Capernaum, a place that had become familiar and comfortable to him. It was his home base now that he had begun his formal ministry. Things had been escalating to say the least. The message, the Good News, was being preached, and people were eager to

Jim Otis

hear it. The touch of God upon broken lives, broken
spirits and broken bodies had certainly had its effect.

Jesus stood up from the rock where he had been
kneeling. He shook off the chill of the third-watch air,
glancing to the east where the sun was just rising. He
stretched and he yawned, and then he chuckled quietly
as he spied Peter running toward him from a distance.
Well, so much for today's solitude.

"There you are, Jesus! Lord, if you could just
coordinate with me before you disappear like this! We
really need to get back into Capernaum. The crowds
are gathering already and everybody, everybody is
looking for you!"

A few of the other ministry team members finally
caught up with Peter and they clustered expectantly
around Jesus, pressing in on him nearly as eagerly
and tight as the huge throngs of people had been doing
lately wherever he went.

"Now here's how I see it," Peter said, urgency and
command tingeing his voice. He diverted the attention
of the little group, barking a few orders, working out
the details of the day. Jesus stepped away, looking off
into the distance as the team plotted their strategies.

"Let's go somewhere else," Jesus said softly. There
was a moment more of chatter, then silence.

"But Lord!" Peter blurted, "The people, the
crowds are in Capernaum. And this is so convenient.
My house is here, my business is here, and we have
everything we need. They'll come to you, Master.
There really isn't any need . . ."

162

"To the nearby villages first," Jesus continued. "So I can preach there also." He caught Peter's eye. "That is why I have come."

Peter knew that look, and he knew that there was no use arguing. There were times when this Messiah had a God-complex.

The next days and weeks were much the same. Throngs of people, Jesus quietly drifting off to solitary places to pray, and Peter had to admit that the Master had been right, in a way. The character of the crowds changed as they moved from village to village and town to town with the Good News. People found them who might never have made it to Capernaum. Jesus' popularity was growing, and Peter wondered if it would ever have reached this apex had they not begun traveling like this.

Then came the day of the Mount. It was a beautiful, gently sloping hillside, not far from Capernaum, actually. In the custom of the great teachers, Jesus ascended the hillside as a great crowd of followers, learners really, came to him. He was seated. His voice carried the News once again, and this sermon for some reason seemed the most comprehensive, the most practical, the most captivating of them all. This Jesus, could he ever preach!

The strong words echoed, they bounced, off the hillside, into the ears of the crowd, bounding, dancing, dangling, flowing down the mount, tripping off into the valleys, dropping down, and bathing even the rocky ravines. His words found their way on that mysterious, supernatural day even into the hearing of a dozing leper. A leper by the name of Simon.

These Words Cannot Be For Me

At first Simon recoiled. These were words such as he could not remember hearing. They were words of . . . blessing. Surely these words were not meant for him. "Blessed, at peace in their ultimate well-being and distinctive spiritual joy, are the poor in spirit, for theirs is the kingdom of heaven."

"Poor in spirit? That's certainly me," though Simon bitterly. "Poor in spirit, poor in body, poor in soul, poor in mind. Just poor, that's sure. Ha! Guess I'm qualified to possess heaven. Guess I already have it, according to those words." He looked, bemused, around his cave. Simon shifted his slight and aching frame on the cave floor, trying to drift off again. But the words kept cascading in, tickling his ears, or at least the oozing, sore flesh where his ears used to be.

". . . for they will be comforted . . . they will inherit the earth . . . they will be filled . . . they will be shown mercy, and *they will see God!*"

What was this all about, Simon wondered. And bitterness aside, he was drawn that day, pulled out of his death cave. He squinted up the rough path toward the road, the road that led to the Mount. "You are the light of the world. You are the salt of the earth!" Simon tried to recall the taste of salt. It had been forever, he guessed, since he had any.

The words kept drawing him out. They were God words. God. Simon didn't know what to think of God, except that for some terrible reason God had forsaken him. But these words, they were sure, they were loving, they were peaceful and yet militant all at once, and the voice compelled him to come. Most of the other lepers from this dismal colony were gone. But where? He found a straggler at the mouth of the cave and asked.

"Didn't you know, Simon? It's the Master. He's a great rabbi. He's been all around here for quite some time now, really. People follow him everywhere. They say he's a great prophet of God. They say his teaching is extraordinary, that it's profound. He speaks words like no man has ever spoken, but more than that, Simon. They say he can heal people. He does miracles."

"Heal them?" Simon whispered. His voice was nearly gone now, his throat a seeping sore. He swallowed constantly.

"Oh yes! He has opened blinded eyes. The lame have walked. One man with a withered arm, why the Rabbi just commanded him to stretch it forth and it was made whole, strong and new, just like that!"

"Just like that," Simon thought. How could this be? "Who . . . who does he heal?" he rasped.

"Well, just about anyone, I suppose. I don't know that he's turned anyone away." He spoke now in a conspiratorial tone, hushed. "Simon, some say that he's the Messiah."

And something broke in Simon. Some kind of chain, some kind of bondage. Broken by a distant memory, a tiny, faithful seed planted deep in his mind. "The Messiah. Didn't it say . . . wouldn't the Messiah heal? Could it be that he might even possibly heal . . . lepers?" Simon had thought to pray for many things, before he had stopped praying altogether, but it had never occurred to him to pray for Messiah to come. And those words, the words, wasn't there something of heaven in those words? So even though his body was sick and weak, his spirit soared as it hadn't soared in years, and he felt it, he felt the force, powerful and rushing in on him: It was hope. It was the hope of something, someone, perhaps, in which once again to have faith.

Journey of a Lifetime

Simon turned. He hobbled toward the path, the same path he hadn't ascended in so very, very long. His eyes were nearly frozen by his disease, but their malfunction couldn't hide the look of determination. Simon was seeing with those diseased eyes. He was seeing so much now. He saw his wife, his beautiful bride. He saw his children, much taller, much more mature. He saw his mother and father, his home and his business, the Temple, his friends. He couldn't let himself see these things before. He had refused to do it, but now they were there. And he knew that he must have them. If nothing else, he knew that he must give it one try. One last try.

"But he's never healed a leper, Simon," the man called after him. "Not that I've ever heard. Simon? Don't be foolish. Never a leper!"

It was amazing how rapidly Simon ascended the path. He didn't take the strength for granted. It was just that he didn't have time to consider its source. He had to use it. He had to climb.

There were many voices now. There was obviously a great crowd, and they were moving. There were voices everywhere, crying out, shouting. It was the first he heard the Name. "Jesus!" they were calling. "Jesus, Son of David, have mercy on me."

"I'll never make it," Simon thought. "He must be leaving now. The crowd, they'll never let me in. They'll throw stones at me like they always do, just to make me keep my distance. I'll never make it," he panted, as he climbed and he rushed all the harder.

He crested the rough embankment at the side of the road, pushing his way through a thorny bush. He knew this would never work, knew it was foolish. A few on the edge of the moving throng spied him there. Simon tried to dodge a neatly aimed stone, but his reflexes had eroded with his flesh and it caught him soundly on the shoulder, nearly knocking him back into the ravine with the force. "Get out of here, you stinking leper!"

Simon scurried to a large boulder and crouched behind it, squinting into the sunlight, searching. He realized with sudden surprise just how filthy and ragged his clothes had become.

Behold Him!

And then he saw him. It had to be him; he was coming Simon's way. The people were everywhere, but they all hovered closely around Jesus. He wasn't anything special to look at, and yet he was. You had to look. Simon blinked. What he was seeing was Love walking. Simon could see that, even from where he was hiding. It was overwhelming. This Love had authority. This Love had purpose. This Love was commanding and yet gentle. Hope was throbbing inside the leper again.

The hope bubbled up, the Love came closer and closer, and Simon lost control. For the first time in years he wept. He wept silently, but with great shaking sobs. He wept for the pain, for the shame, for the loss. He just crouched there, shaking, aching, bleeding, oozing, and weeping. Hot tears washing dead eyes.

The Faithful Leap

And then he did it. The leper, Simon the Leper, gathered every shard of strength he had left for one final, great leap. He leapt out from behind that rock so fast, so surprisingly that no one could stop him. He leapt and he prayed and he landed there in the road, painfully on his knees, the flesh tearing away, but it didn't matter. He landed, miracle of miracles, right in front of him. He landed directly in the path of Jesus. The dirty, decaying leper put himself flatly in front of the Lord of life.

Jesus stopped. The crowd, shocked at this sudden appearing drew back quickly from the leper, even Peter and the ministry team, leaving Jesus and Simon in the middle of a circling wall of humanity.

Jesus fixed his attention on Simon alone. It became absolutely still and silent. Simon struggled again to focus his nearly lifeless eyes, and then he saw it. He saw that he was right. In that instant he knew that he had reason to hope, because now he could see Jesus' eyes. The leper drew in a hurting breath. The crowd was straining to hear him. Surely Jesus would put this off-fall of humanity, this ragged, repulsive sinner, held together only by filth in his place.

Simon strained to speak the words, none truer, none more perfectly phrased, none more divinely inspired than these: "If . . . you . . . are willing . . . you can make me clean."

As forced and as low as his leprous throat would utter these words they still seemed to come out strong, even to echo as he spoke.

And Then There Was Peter

Divine transactions happened every day, many, many times a day, wherever Jesus went. But something unusual occurred here. This went out of control. Peter saw it first. It just coursed up out of Jesus and spilled over like a powerful, rushing stream, and then it was flowing and pounding like the rapids of a river. It was unbridled and certainly unpredictable. It was something to be feared. Peter knew this, because he knew Jesus. He had never known a stronger man, and yet this man, this strongest model of divinity had lost control and was being driven by absolute compassion.

Before Peter could imagine it, Jesus was reaching out to this leper.

"I am willing," Jesus said, and Peter stood frozen, wanting to act but unable, wanting to cry out, but he couldn't. He could only think it, think it desperately, urgently and hope that Jesus would somehow pick up on it. "Stop! Stop it! You can't touch a leper! Oh, Jesus, stop it! You've got a responsibility before God not to do this thing. You, of all men, must remain clean. Look at this ministry we've got. You'll ruin it. You'll regret it, and I've never seen you regret anything in your life. You'll sacrifice it all, and for what? For this leper? Think, Jesus! Come on. Get your head out of your heart and use some reason, for heaven's sake!" But all that came out of Peter's mouth was a grunt. It was a dismal, guttural grunt, quite pitiful, really.

Jesus paused for just an instant, turning to look at Peter, and Peter even could sense the Love. Jesus continued his reach. He not only reached, but he grasped Simon the Leper, right on a leper's wound, on an open, bloody sore. With ultimate authority he spoke the words, "Be clean!"

As Jesus turned from Peter his loving eyes met those of Simon and a love-flow began. That leper's body, but oh, so much more significantly his spirit, his heart, his soul were all restored.

At once the disease fled. The sores disappeared. The foul odor dissipated. Simon's eyebrows and eyelashes reappeared. His hoarse voice was made strong, as that of one who could once again call out loudly and clearly in the marketplace. The mixture of numbness and pain was gone as Simon felt, yes! He could *feel* it, the rush of life-giving, cleansing blood pounding out to his very extremities. Extremities! New fingers, new toes! He was Simon the Leper, but he was Simon the Leper made clean and whole.

It was interesting, then, because on that particular day no one even dared to think that in this act of touching Jesus had become unclean. Only cleaner, in fact; purer, more righteous, more holy. Only more loving, more awesome and more inviting to them all. Even Peter really saw it then, but most especially Simon.

On that day everyone learned that there was One who could and would touch lepers, recreating their ravaged bodies. That touch transformed Simon. He became a new creation of God, fully restored. He had a new perspective, and his thinking, his feeling, his actions and his words would never be the same again. For the rest of his life on earth, and today in heaven, Simon has never ceased looking, gazing on Jesus. He has never changed his focus. He quit looking at the obstacles that day, even at the crowd, even at the healing of his own body. He focused on Jesus, the Author and Finisher of his faith, and his focus has never wavered.[76]

Chapter Eighteen
Would Anyone Choose A World Without His Touch?

The Thanksgiving Prayer

A four year-old boy was asked to say a prayer before Thanksgiving dinner. The family bowed and he began his prayer, thanking God for all his friends. Then he thanked God for Mom and Dad, Grandma, Grandpa, and all his aunts and uncles. Then he began to thank God for the food. He gave thanks for the turkey, the dressing, the fruit salad, the cranberry sauce, the pies, and the cakes. He thanked God mightily and particularly for the Cool Whip, adding a slight tremble to his voice as he had heard his Grandpa do whenever he offered an especially important prayer.

Then he paused. After a long silence, he looked up and said, "Mom, if I thank God for the broccoli and for my sister, won't he just *know* I'm lying?"

Sometimes my thanks for the grace in and under which I subsist isn't much better than a lie. It's not a careful or considered thanks. It's thanks on the run, maybe on the fly. If I'm not careful, I can find myself trapped in a thankless day. We're pretty busy to be worried about giving thanks. I'm working to develop a more sincere, constant gratitude; something genuine. I know it's much more for my benefit than for God's sense of fulfillment that I should develop this. Giving thanks improves us; it doesn't gratify God, other than in the fact that he knows we advance our

172

understanding of his grace whenever we offer thanks. But I think there are deeper reasons than just busyness that underlie the general ungratefulness of the average human heart.

A Graceless, Self-Sufficient World

I think of it as a matter of how the world sees itself, and how it believes it originated. You see, if our self-sufficient world was established and came to be inhabited by chance and not Creation, it's nothing more than a bank of resources. If that's the case, the world becomes a thing to be used, exploited, manipulated, built upon and then torn down and built bigger again. There's nothing for which to be thankful in a world into which we stumbled, and then survived to tame and to shape by ourselves, by our own ingenuity, our own clever inventiveness, our own brute will and strength. Why should we be thankful for that? And what should we say? "Thank me very much for my self-sufficient world?"

No Satisfaction

There are some big problems in a world like that, however. The first thing we find in a self-sufficient world is that we're stuck with it, forced to extract whatever fulfillment we can from a pitifully insufficient source. Have you ever written a check that bounced? Insufficient funds can't be drawn upon, can they? This world bank of resources is insufficient and graceless to the deepest human needs. But if we choose to ignore the Creator, it is from this insufficient world alone that we must attempt to withdraw our satisfaction. This world, then, must deliver on its own promises. Mick Jagger made the perfect commentary on that unreasonable expectation: "I can't get no satisfaction." There is no blood coming from turnips, and there is no capital reserve in a bankrupt system.

A Transient World

The next problem we find is the transience of a graceless, self-sufficient world. The empty promise of a transient world is what sends us scurrying off to scrap and toil beyond reason for more things which have, above all else, nothing but a shelf-life attached to them; a "best used before" date, beyond which there is . . . what?

For the self-sufficient, this disappearing, consumable world becomes the environment in which we must not only find satisfaction but also our significance. That's a serious frustration, because God has set eternity in our hearts, and yet we have, by our own definition of human life and the nature of the universe, declared it all to be finite. We've made it terminal. Having come from nothing, it exists for a short, momentous burst, and dissipates into the dark night, extinguished, snuffed out.

When you and your world base your origins in pure chance, the only anticipation with which you are left is for the end. An end that relentlessly, impartially, irreducibly, unforgivingly approaches at a breakneck pace. You cannot withdraw significance from that bank account. The only balance it has remaining is ruin, not significance.

"Good," in such a world as that, becomes purely a relative thing, and seems desirable only to the extent that it somehow benefits oneself. "Love" becomes vain and self-serving. Silly, temporal words, that's all.

An Incapable World

Such a world is also incapable. It cannot respond. It cannot in any sense minister to the hurts that it inflicts, nor to the hurts that we inflict upon one another. It can't "meet needs." It's senseless and insensible.

It got very cold the other day, out of season, and that's how the thought of an insufficient, insignificant, incapable, immovable world leaves me, but that's the realm into which such a large percentage of humanity has placed itself and in which it remains, bowing down to a tough, terminal world and to that which we have chipped out of it.

A Thankless Idolater

If I were the product of such a thing, of course I'd be ungrateful! The Bible has sort of an odd take on such behavior: It's called *idolatry*. The idolater has no thanks in his heart other than to the idol that he has made, and that idol only, always represents the tiny "godlet" that man has made himself to be, and for which he is forced to settle. The idolater is thankless for that, and I don't blame him!

May I ask if you're practicing genuine thanksgiving at any point in your daily life? Do you have genuine thanks in your heart, rising up worshipfully to the one true God who is so much greater than yourself? Are you in any sense grateful for his grace? Are you grateful for his gift? Or does it all, along with him, go unacknowledged? You see, the only response for one who has recognized the true gift-nature of God's grace is thanksgiving.

The Apostle Paul, whom we met in the first chapter, gives us some guidelines for the Christian observance of Holy Communion, or the Lord's Supper as we often call it. Paul says we must *"flee from idolatry. Is not the cup of thanksgiving for which we give thanks a participation in the blood of Christ? And is not the bread that we break a participation in the body of Christ?"*[77]

Yet God So Loved

Paul wants us to understood that *". . . God so loved the world that he gave his one and only Son, that whoever believes in him shall not perish but have eternal life."*[78]

God loves the world. God *so loves* this bankrupt old world that he *gave*. He not only Created, he not only populated, he not only sustains, but he gave himself that we might NOT perish from off the face of a terminal, graceless globe, but that we might have eternal life. He came, he lived, he died, he conquered, that we might find sufficiency, that we might discover significance, that we might find hope and help in our time of need. God so loves this world that he gave us reason to remember, reason to drink, reason to eat to his glory, reason to grasp *"the cup of thanksgiving, for which we give thanks."*

God so loves this world, the real world, not the other world that we were talking about, that he has chosen to redeem it. In commentary on the French mathematician and philosopher Pascal's sayings offered the insight that, "The believer can have no pride because we are united to God wholly by grace, not by nature or by our own worthiness. And yet we have no despair because we are miserable only by our fall into sin, not by our origin and our destiny, both of which are divine. [So] to be children of Adam is both greatness enough to raise any head and shame enough to lower it."[79] And it is cause enough not to be thanklessly idolatrous, but to be exceedingly thankful to this same personal God, so full of grace that we have cause for eternal wonder.

A World That Stands to Reason

A redeemable world like this makes sense. The world under God makes sense. It winds up and not down, it gathers significance as it goes, it gains momentum rather than losing it. The world under God stands to reason. We can withdraw from its bank account reason enough to serve God and to serve others; to serve one another, our families, our communities, our church, our nation, and our very world itself. The world under God becomes larger. It becomes worthy of such a thing as sacrifice. It takes on meaning in our coming, in our abiding and, yes, even in our going. Perhaps especially in our going.

The challenges of the world under God take on such sweet anticipation because they have a meaning and a hope that is so much greater than self-gratification, or even the common good for that matter, because meeting the challenges of the world under God gives birth to significance framed in eternity.

A Responding World

The world under God responds. It moves, it yields, it cares. That's why the psalmist could say to God, "You are with me in my times of trouble." *"You keep track of all my sorrows. You have collected all my tears in your bottle. You have recorded each one in your book." (Psalm 56:8 NLT.)* That doesn't sound immovable to me.

It's why the psalmist could say, "You are with me in my times of despair." *"I will be glad and rejoice in your love, for you [have seen] my affliction and [you have known] the anguish of my soul." (Psalm 31:7 NIV.)* That doesn't sound detached.

It's why he could even say, "You are with me in my foolish mistakes." *"You know my folly, O God; my guilt is not hidden from you." (Psalm 69:5 NIV.)* And yet you do not cast me away. And yet you find me precious, redeemable, and worthy. That doesn't sound unyielding.

It's why the psalmist could say, "You are with me in my very humanness." *"For [you] remember how we are formed, [you] remember that we are dust."* (Psalm *103:14 NIV.)* You remember full well that you did the making! That doesn't sound unforgiving, does it?[80]

At Long Last Thankful

For this world, this world under God; *for* it, *in* it, *through* it, we can at last give thanks to the God who so loves the world. And in giving thanks we acknowledge not mere chance, but the world's Creator, our Source. We acknowledge not senselessness, but the hope of significance we find in him. We acknowledge not insufficiency, but the Substance of the gift that has been given to us, the gift of redemption, the gift of purpose, the gift of hope. In giving thanks we practice a form of worship. We cleave to our Creator and to the meaning we find only in him. And we submit to his existence, to his Sovereignty, and to his world-conquering love.

God's Passionate Appeal to Win Your Heart

God has made his appeal, through his golden Creation, through the plan of redemption, through his Son, through his Cross, through the power that took him beyond. It is that same power that he offers to invest in your life. God so loves YOU; can you then begin to consider drinking the cup of thanksgiving with me, by honoring him with your life? If so, in this next all-important chapter we shall consider walking together down life's most wondrous path. It's the path that I like to call *The Clear Path Home*, and we'll discover exactly how to walk it.

Chapter Nineteen
The Clear Path Home: God's Simple Answer to Life's Greatest Question

Having Come This Far

You've stuck with it this far, and that's no small thing. You've wrestled with the idea of the personal and the corporate sin of mankind, which is not a palatable or an easy task. You've grappled with the idea of God as Creator and as the Sovereign Lord of the universe, which is no mean concept. You've allowed room in your mind for the Essential Assumptions, for the purpose of giving God a fair hearing, and that is a prodigious undertaking in itself.

So now there comes this moment of reckoning. God has deliberately set you at the entrance to this path. It is the Clear Path Home. It is mapped out in Scripture and God is beckoning you to walk it, to take it Home. He is beckoning you to come to him on this path, and to make his path *your* path. Having come this far, why not consider this final appeal?

The Spirit and the bride say, "Come!" And let him who hears say, "Come!" Whoever is thirsty, let him come; and whoever wishes, let him take the free gift of the water of life.[81]

Milestones for the Journey

Every journey begins with the first step, continues with each successive step, and is completed by the last step, and this one is no different. This is a path that can be walked. This is a journey of completion. You can take the final step into the arms of the patient, beckoning God who awaits you. And when you take that final step, both the journey and your *self* are completed.

There are milestones of realization on this journey. It is, as we have agreed throughout this book, more of a process than it is an event. But it is a process that is marked along the way with milestones that commemorate and celebrate your progress. We have covered this path, actually, in the pages that have preceded these, perhaps with the exception of the mechanics of commitment. So here is a synopsis of some key Scriptures that comprise the path, and here are the final details of God's passionate appeal to win your heart. Each concept serves as a mile marker. As you may guess, I am tempted to embellish this presentation, but it seems wise to allow God to speak for himself through his written Word, directly to your heart.

Milestone 1
Let's assume there is a God and you can know him through faith.

And without faith it is impossible to please God, because anyone who comes to him must believe that he exists and that he rewards those who earnestly seek him.
Hebrews 11:6 NIV

Milestone 2
God's existence is evident to all.

For since the creation of the world God's invisible qualities - his eternal power and divine nature - have been clearly seen, being understood from what has been made, so that men are without excuse.
Romans 1:20 NIV

Milestone 3
Humanity is God's good creation.

1 In the beginning God created the heavens and the earth. 27 So God created man in his own image, in the image of God he created him; male and female he created them. 28(a) God blessed them and said to them, "Be fruitful and increase in number; fill the earth and subdue it." 31(a) God saw all that he had made, and it was very good.
Genesis 1:1, 27-28(a), 31(a) NIV

Milestone 4
God created humans as eternal beings with the "light" of spiritual knowledge, but also with clear boundaries.

1 In the beginning was the Word, and the Word was with God, and the Word was God. 2 He was with God in the beginning. 3 Through him all things were made; without him nothing was made that has been made. 4 In him was life, and that life was the light of men.
John 1:1-4 NIV

". . . you must not eat from the tree of the knowledge of good and evil, for when you eat of it you will surely die."
Genesis 2:17 NIV

Milestone 5
When man chose to commit sin, he ruined his relationship with God

6 When the woman saw that the fruit of the tree was good for food and pleasing to the eye, and also desirable for gaining wisdom, she took some and ate it. She also gave some to her husband, who was with her, and he ate it. 8 Then the man and his wife heard the sound of the LORD God as he was walking in the garden in the cool of the day, and they hid from the LORD God among the trees of the garden.
Genesis 3:6, 8 NIV

Milestone 6
Sin is a universal and personal thing. As with all people, you too have willfully committed sin.

22(b) There is no difference, 23 for all have sinned and fall short of the glory of God,
Romans 3:22(b)-23 NIV

If you, O LORD, kept a record of sins, O LORD, who could stand?
Psalm 130:3 NIV

Milestone 7
Your sin separates you from God.

But your iniquities have separated you from your God; your sins have hidden his face from you, so that he will not hear.
Isaiah 59:2 NIV

Milestone 8
Sin enslaves and controls people.

Jesus replied, "I tell you the truth, everyone who sins is a slave to sin."
John 8:34 NIV

20 But the wicked are like the tossing sea, which cannot rest, whose waves cast up mire and mud. 21 "There is no peace," says my God, "for the wicked."
Isaiah 57:20-21 NIV

Milestone 9
Sin is so serious and so offends the righteousness and justice of God that it results in spiritual and physical death with unending destruction.

For the wages of sin is death, . . .
Romans 6:23(a) NIV

For every living soul belongs to me, the father as well as the son - both alike belong to me. The soul who sins is the one who will die.
Ezekiel 18:4 NIV

8 He will punish those who do not know God and do not obey the gospel of our Lord Jesus. 9 They will be punished with everlasting destruction and shut out from the presence of the Lord and from the majesty of his power.
2 Thessalonians 1:8-9 NIV

Milestone 10

Although you are separated from God, you have a longing for immortality and desire to know Him.

He has made everything beautiful in its time. He has also set eternity in the hearts of men . . .
Ecclesiastes 3:11(a) NIV

I want to know Christ and the power of his resurrection
Philippians 3:10(a) NIV

Milestone 11

God doesn't want you to die in your sin, nor does he desire to punish you. He is seeking you out to restore the relationship he once had with mankind, but which was lost because of our choice to sin.

For the Son of Man came to seek and to save what was lost.
Luke 19:10 NIV

But the LORD God called to the man, "Where are you?"
Genesis 3:9 NIV

". . . but the gift of God is eternal life in Christ Jesus our Lord."
Romans 6:23(a) NIV

3 This is good, and pleases God our Savior, 4 who wants all men to be saved and to come to a knowledge of the truth.
1 Timothy 2:3-4 NIV

Milestone 12

Although you are a sinner, Jesus is the sinner's friend!

10   While Jesus was having dinner at Matthew's house, many tax collectors and "sinners" came and ate with him and his disciples.   11 When the [religious leaders] saw this they asked his disciples, "Why does your teacher eat with tax collectors and 'sinners'?"
Matthew 9:10-11 NIV

35 Jesus went through all the towns and villages, teaching in their synagogues, preaching the good news of the kingdom and healing every disease and sickness. 36 When he saw the crowds, he had compassion on them, because they were harassed and helpless, like sheep without a shepherd.
Matthew 9:35-36 NIV

Milestone 13

Jesus personally paid the price for your sin, so He could give you salvation as a gift.

He himself bore our sins in his body on the tree, so that we might die to sins and live for righteousness; by his wounds you have been healed.
1 Peter 2:24 NIV

*8 For it is by grace you have been saved, **through faith - and this not from yourselves, it is the gift of God** - 9 not by works, so that no one can boast.*
Ephesians 2:8-9 NIV

*For the wages of sin is death, but **the gift** of God is eternal life in Christ Jesus our Lord.*
Romans 6:23 NIV

Milestone 14

Jesus' blood, shed on the Cross of Calvary, was the "perfect, imperishable sacrifice" for your freedom.

18 For you know that it was not with perishable things such as silver or gold that you were redeemed from the empty way of life handed down to you from your forefathers, 19 but with the precious blood of Christ, a lamb without blemish or defect. 20 He was chosen before the creation of the world, but was revealed in these last times for your sake. 21 Through him you believe in God, who raised him from the dead and glorified him, and so your faith and hope are in God.
1 Peter 1:18-21 NIV

Milestone 15

In love, God chose to do for you that which you are powerless to do on your own.

16 "For God so loved the world that he gave his one and only Son, that whoever believes in him shall not perish but have eternal life. 17 For God did not send his Son into the world to condemn the world, but to save the world through him."
John 3:16-17 NIV

6 You see, at just the right time, when we were still powerless, Christ died for the ungodly. 8 But God demonstrates his own love for us in this: While we were still sinners, Christ died for us.
Romans 5:6, 8 NIV

Milestone 16
The life Jesus offers you is amazingly full.

"The thief comes only to steal and kill and destroy; I have come that they may have life, and have it to the full."

John 10:10 NIV

8 Though you have not seen him, you love him; and even though you do not see him now, you believe in him and are filled with an inexpressible and glorious joy, 9 for you are receiving the goal of your faith, the salvation of your souls.

1 Peter 1:8-9 NIV

Milestone 17

Jesus is God's only "way and means" of obtaining eternal life.

Jesus answered, "I am the way and the truth and the life. No one comes to the Father except through me."

John 14:6 NIV

For there is one God and one mediator between God and men, the man Christ Jesus, 6 who gave himself as a ransom for all men-the testimony given in its proper time.

1 Timothy 2:5-6 NIV

Milestone 18

The event by which you enter into eternal life is so significant and so transformational that Jesus depicts it as being "born again."

5 Jesus answered, "I tell you the truth, no one can enter the kingdom of God unless he is born of water and the Spirit. 6 Flesh gives birth to flesh, but the Spirit gives birth to spirit. 7 You should not be surprised at my saying, 'You must be born again.'"
John 3:5-7 NIV

Milestone 19

Your simple part in being "born again" is to choose to submit to God by placing your faith in Jesus Christ.

25 Jesus said to her, "I am the resurrection and the life. He who believes in me will live, even though he dies; 26 and whoever lives and believes in me will never die. Do you believe this?" 27 "Yes, Lord," she told him, "I believe that you are the Christ, the Son of God, who was to come into the world."
John 11:25-27 NIV

They replied, "Believe in the Lord Jesus, and you will be saved - you and your household."
Acts 16:31 NIV

Milestone 20

As you place your faith in Christ, you make a "confession" of your sin, which means you "agree with God" regarding the seriousness of sin, and admit that you have personally committed sin. In essence, you take the necessary step of claiming personal responsibility for your sin.

8 If we claim to be without sin, we deceive ourselves and the truth is not in us. 9 If we confess our

sins, he is faithful and just and will forgive us our sins and purify us
from all unrighteousness. 10 If we claim we have not sinned, we make him out to be a liar and his word has no place in our lives.
1 John 1:8-10 NIV

Milestone 21

As you place your faith in Christ you also experience repentance, which is a God-inspired sorrow for your sin. Part of repentance is your willing resolve, with the full expectation of completion, to turn away from your old life as God gives you the help you need to do so.

Repent, [change your mind!] then, and turn to God, so that your sins may be wiped out, that times of refreshing may come from the Lord,
Acts 3:19 NIV
For if you live according to the sinful nature, you will die; but if by the Spirit you put to death the misdeeds of the body, you will live,
Romans 8:13 NIV

Milestone 22

By faith you are then able to reorient your life as your heart and spirit are made new.
30 Repent! Turn away from all your offenses; then sin will not be your downfall. 31 Rid yourselves of all the offenses you have committed, and get a new heart and a new spirit. Why will you die, O house of Israel?

32 For I take no pleasure in the death of anyone, declares the Sovereign LORD. Repent and live!
Ezekiel 18:30(b)-32 NIV

26 I will give you a new heart and put a new spirit in you; I will remove from you your heart of stone and give you a heart of flesh. 27 And I will put my Spirit in you and move you to follow my decrees and be careful to keep my laws. 28 You will live in the land I gave your forefathers; you will be my people, and I will be your God. 29 I will save you from all your uncleanness.
Ezekiel 36:26-29 NIV

Milestone 23
When you believe in Jesus Christ you are virtually "reborn" as God's own child.

12 Yet to all who received him, to those who believed in his name, he gave the right to become children of God - 13 children born not of natural descent, nor of human decision or a husband's will, but born of God.
John 1:12-13 NIV

Milestone 24
When you believe in Christ you open yourself up to having intimate fellowship with him.

20 "Here I am! I stand at the door and knock. If anyone hears my voice and opens the door, I will come in and eat with him, and he with me."
Revelation 3:20 NIV

Milestone 25

God invites you to come and experience life in Christ Jesus through faith.

The Spirit and the bride say, "Come!" And let him who hears say, "Come!" Whoever is thirsty, let him come; and whoever wishes, let him take the free gift of the water of life.
Revelation 22:17 NIV

Milestone 26

You will choose either to accept or reject God's invitation to life.

*This day I call heaven and earth as witnesses against you that I have set before you life and death, blessings and curses. **Now choose life,** so that you and your children may live 20 and that you may love the LORD your God, listen to his voice, and hold fast to him. For the LORD is your life*
Deuteronomy 30:19-20(a) NIV

Milestone 27

The moment you choose life by putting your faith in Jesus Christ, God keeps His Word and you receive His gift of salvation.

*9 That if you confess with your mouth, "Jesus is Lord," and **believe** in your heart that God raised him from the dead, **you will be saved.** 10 For it is with your heart that you **believe and are justified,** and it is with your mouth that you confess and are saved. 13 for, **"Everyone who calls on the name of the Lord will be saved."***
Romans 10:9-10, 13 NIV

Milestone 28

A marvelous act of "re-creation" happens when you believe in Jesus Christ.

Therefore, if anyone is in Christ, he is a new creation; the old has gone, the new has come!
2 Corinthians 5:17 NIV

[nothing else by way of religious rituals or symbols] means anything; what counts is a new creation.
Galatians 6:15 NIV

Milestone 29

You can have the full assurance that you have eternal life in Christ.

13 I write these things to you who believe in the name of the Son of God so that you may know that you have eternal life. 14 This is the confidence we have in approaching God: that if we ask anything according to his will, he hears us.
1 John 5:13-14 NIV

But now in Christ Jesus you who once were far away have been brought near through the blood of Christ.
Ephesians 2:13 NIV

Milestone 30

You can be certain that you have been adopted by God Himself, with all of the rights and privileges of a child and an heir.

4 But when the time had fully come, God sent his Son, born of a woman, born under law, 5 to redeem those under law, that we might receive the full rights of sons. 6 Because you are sons, God sent the Spirit of his Son into our hearts, the Spirit who calls out, "Abba, Father." 7 So you are no

longer a slave, but a son; and since you are a son, God has made you also an heir.

Galatians 4:4-7 NIV

Chapter Twenty
Simon the Leper and the Case of the Broken Bottle

"Now to him who is able to do immeasurably more than all we ask or imagine, according to his power that is at work within us, to him be glory in the church and in Christ Jesus throughout all generations, forever and ever. Amen"

Ephesians 3:20-21 NIV

Guess Who's Coming to Dinner?

The noonday sun was bright and the sky was a deep middle-eastern blue on that perfect day in Bethany, a tiny village positioned a little less than two miles outside of Jerusalem. Bethany was a hub of activity just now and a bold statement was being made.

There was a celebratory feast going on in that village, and there were two honored guests who were the toast and the talk of the town. The first was Jesus. Now in his third year of ministry, Jesus had become renowned. True, he had experienced his troubles, too. The Jewish religious leaders weren't fond of him at all. In fact, they were seeking a way to kill him.

The second guest was Jesus' dear friend and handiwork, Lazarus. "Handiwork" because just a few days before this Lazarus was dead. He was not just dead for a moment and then resuscitated, but he was dead for four days. He had been wrapped up in seventy pounds of spices, resin-like goo and strips of cloth to preserve his body, but Lazarus was rotting, stinking dead. He had been locked-in-the-tomb dead. Then Jesus came and raised Lazarus back to wholeness, freshness and amazing life. Factually, Jesus let Lazarus die. Yet this, his final miracle, would be his most intimate, dramatic and illustrative. Jesus had the power over life and death, and he proved it. How extensive was that power the people really had yet to see, but see they would, and soon enough.

Naturally, Lazarus became an instant celebrity. Everyone wanted to have him over for dinner. Who wouldn't? If you could score Jesus and Lazarus together, well, that would be the epitome of the social century. You could dine out on that story for the rest of your life.

It Had to be at Simon's House

Yes, everyone wanted to throw a feast for Jesus, and everyone wanted to sit down with Lazarus, but Jesus had selected one special person for that honor, perhaps very carefully. One who had been nearly as dead and probably had suffered more physical decay than Lazarus. The feast would take place at the home of Simon. That would be Simon *the Leper*.

Simon loved his name. Once he had hated it, but now he loved the contradictory nature of it. His name was like an inside joke between himself and God. Simon the Leper was now, by the power of Jesus the Christ, Simon the Clean. Nearly three years ago Jesus had healed Simon the Leper, bringing him back from the brink of certain death. Simon had been pronounced clean and pure by the awe-smitten priests the same day Jesus had touched him. He had been readmitted to the Temple and to life. Simon's family was restored to him and he to they, and all had become believers in Jesus and fiercely devoted followers. How could they not, given Simon's irrefutable testimony?

The Awesome Assemblage

As the people gathered it was truly an awesome assemblage. Jesus himself. Lazarus. Simon the Leper. They were eating in the home of a leper!

The feast was winding down when something unusual happened, although no one who followed Jesus for any time at all considered much of anything to be unusual anymore. Mary, the sister of Lazarus, approached Jesus. She was cradling a delicate alabaster jar in her hands as she knelt at Jesus' feet. This jar held the most precious fragrance known in the world at that time, and represented Mary's life savings. She could retire on the contents of that jar.

Seeing her there, kneeling, and knowing the value of the jar, the crowd grew silent. In the stillness of that poignant moment everyone heard a distinct, tinkling snap as Mary broke the jar at its neck and the expensive ointment began to flow. Normally this pure nard would have been used sparingly to anoint the head of an honored guest, but anointing the head was the prerogative of a host, and Mary chose to do the work of the lowliest servant. She would only anoint Jesus' feet. And to be sparing was not an option where her Master was concerned; rather, Mary would spend it all. She would lavish him with ointment, holding nothing back.

The fragrance wafted through the room, over all the people, rich, rich nard, finally pouring out of the windows and into the breeze. It was as if the whole village was enveloped in that wonderful aroma.

True, some complained, but not Jesus. He knew the deep symbolism in Mary's ministry. Lazarus approved of his sister's act, even as Mary took down her hair, something that a respectable woman never did in public, and used it to dry Jesus' feet. Mary was willing to sacrifice her respectability to honor her Lord. Simon the Leper thought it perfectly appropriate, and would remember Mary's worshipful sacrifice long past the scent that would linger in his house for a number of days.

The Case of the Broken Bottle

A leper healed and restored. A dead man raised. A woman willing to spend her retirement in one extraordinary measure. That is the power of Jesus. The case of the broken bottle was more than just that. The bottle was a mere gesture, a small thanks for the lavish grace that Jesus had given to these participants. It was a case of total restoration. It was a case of total thanks. It was a case of total commitment on the eve of Jesus' total investment in the salvation of mankind.

Simon walked out of the house for a few quiet moments, thinking, praying, thanking God for what he sensed was the unique privilege of knowing Jesus. Here he was, a leper who had been changed by the One who touches lepers. Here he was, a leper who had been touched by the One who changes lives.

As Simon prayed, he prayed not only in gratitude for himself, but also for the souls of those who should know this Savior. He thought of other broken lives. He thought how Jesus would be broken himself to bring the mending that only God can bring. He thought of other proud and self-sufficient hearts. He thought how Jesus would willingly empty himself of all dignity and would be utterly humbled for their salvation. He prayed for others in his extended family, for friends and neighbors. He prayed for his fellow countrymen. He prayed for the people of his day and for the people of all the days of grace yet to come. He prayed that they would hear and they would heed God's ultimate, passionate appeal to win their hearts. He prayed that they would step with purpose onto the Clear Path Home.[82]

Chapter Twenty-One
The Final Commitment

This is Your Moment

You have heard God's appeal. He asks you now to choose. This is your special moment. It is the moment of your visitation.

So from now on we regard no one from a worldly point of view. Though we once regarded Christ in this way, we do so no longer. Therefore, if anyone is in Christ, he is a new creation; the old has gone, the new has come!

All this is from God, who reconciled us to himself through Christ and gave us the ministry of reconciliation: that God was reconciling the world to himself in Christ, not counting men's sins against them. And he has committed to us the message of reconciliation.

We are therefore Christ's ambassadors, as though God were making his appeal through us. We implore you on Christ's behalf: Be reconciled to God. God made him who had no sin to be sin for us, so that in him we might become the righteousness of God.

As God's fellow workers we urge you not to receive God's grace in vain. For he says,

"In the time of my favor I heard you, and in the day of salvation I helped you."

I tell you, now is the time of God's favor, now is the day of salvation.

- 2 Corinthians 5:16-6:2

You have heard the arguments, but at this choosing point God leaves no more room for arguments. He wants you to make one last assumption, because it is the total truth: God has given you all the facts. He has given you all the substance that he knows is required for you to make an informed choice about your relationship with him. He has given you everything you need in order to make this critical decision.

There can be no baby steps at this point; we're talking about taking a plunge. Saving faith is not a tentative thing. It has the idea of jumping off a cliff and expecting God to catch you, not the idea of gingerly and rapidly sticking your finger in a pot and pulling it out again to see if the water is cold or hot. The purposeful exercise of saving faith is the very definition of full commitment. Faith is not doubt. Faith has no expectation of turning back.

There is a time for everything,
and a season for every activity under heaven:
a time to be born and a time to die,
a time to plant and a time to uproot,
a time to kill and a time to heal,
a time to tear down and a time to build,
a time to weep and a time to laugh,
a time to mourn and a time to dance,
a time to scatter stones and a time to gather them,
a time to embrace and a time to refrain,
a time to search and a time to give up,
a time to keep and a time to throw away,

a time to tear and a time to mend,
a time to be silent and a time to speak,
a time to love and a time to hate,
a time for war and a time for peace.
- Ecclesiastes 3:1-8

There is a time to consider and a time to choose. There is a time to doubt and a time to trust. There is a time to wait and a time to act.

All in the Balance

There is a great deal hanging in the balance now. There is the matter of your destiny. God compels you to choose life. Naturally, a refusal to do so is to choose death by default, for with God there is no middle ground, there is no fence on which to perch.

Have you ever watched a movie where someone is headed to sure destruction, but they just blunder on anyway? Sometimes the character is placed in a situation where they clearly could not know, and that's one thing. But at other times they should know, it's just that they choose to ignore the facts or they fail to process the available information. And so you find yourself shouting at the screen,

"Don't open that door!" or, "Don't go down those stairs! *What are you thinking?!*"

In a sense, that is what God is communicating to us through the wisdom of the following Proverbs. He has set before us everything we need, he has made his appeal, he has issued his warnings. God has said his piece. Do you choose to ignore the facts? Could you possibly neglect to process the information? This passage of Scripture is laden with truth pertinent to this moment:

The plans of the foolish and the thought of foolishness are sin, and the scoffer is an abomination to men.

If you faint in the day of adversity, your strength is small.

Deliver those who are drawn away to death, and those who totter to the slaughter, hold them back [from their doom].

If you [profess ignorance and] say, Behold, we did not know this, does not He Who weighs and ponders the heart perceive and consider it? And He Who guards your life, does not He know it? And shall not He render to [you and] every man according to his works?

My son, eat honey, because it is good, and the drippings of the honeycomb are sweet to your taste.

So shall you know skillful and godly Wisdom to be thus to your life; if you find it, then shall there be a future and a reward, and your hope and expectation shall not be cut off.

-    Proverbs 24:9-14 The Amplified Bible

What Are You Going to Do With It?

A number of years ago some people introduced me to the concept of downsizing and bartering. Someone had written a self-published book and was going around doing seminars on building net worth. His idea was that we all have things we don't need any more lying around gathering dust. We should take those things and convert them to cash, or, better yet, use them to barter for better things for which we might actually have a use. He had a corny title for his book, which is probably why his system didn't catch on wildly and why he faded into obscurity. He called it, *"Whatchagonnadowithwhatchagot?"*

A corny title, but I remember the concept to this day. And the question is a good one: *What are you going to do with what you have?* God's passionate appeal to you, based upon all that he has invested in you, all that he has given you, all that he has taught you, is for you to give him your heart. He wants you to come home. He has set you on the Clear Path. Will you choose life, that you may live with him forever? Will you eat the honey, because it is good and it is sweet? He has set it before you; he has given it to you. Now what will you do with what you have?

What Can I Say?

We come to God in different ways, but all in response to the same information. Some walk the aisle at the end of a church service and kneel at an altar. That's symbolic and can be powerful, while others feel it is manipulative and improper. Some walk across a stadium field and stand in front of a platform. Some, in the throes of desperation, cry out to God from the bed where they have been tossing and turning in the dark of night, with a deeper darkness yet in their soul. Some breathe a quiet prayer on an afternoon walk, inspired by Creation and their longing to know the Creator.

How and where you come to God is not the issue. *That* you come to God is the pivot point of life. Some folks get hung up on what to say. That isn't the issue either. What you are purposing in your heart is God's concern, not your capability to sound contrite or religious or theological. Here are some ideas from Scripture that might help:

To some who were confident of their own righteousness and looked down on everybody else, Jesus told this parable:

"Two men went up to the temple to pray, one a Pharisee and the other a tax collector. The Pharisee stood up and prayed about himself: 'God, I thank you that I am not like other men-robbers, evildoers, adulterers-or even like this tax collector. I fast twice a week and give a tenth of all I get.'

"But the tax collector stood at a distance. He would not even look up to heaven, but beat his breast and said, 'God, have mercy on me, a sinner.'

"I tell you that this man, rather than the other, went home justified before God. For everyone who exalts himself will be humbled, and he who humbles himself will be exalted."

- Luke 18:9-14 NIV

The crucible for silver and the furnace for gold, but the LORD tests the heart.
- Proverbs 17:3 NIV

". . . .But if you can do anything, take pity on us and help us."

" 'If you can'?" said Jesus. "Everything is possible for him who believes."

Immediately the boy's father exclaimed, "I do believe; help me overcome my unbelief!"

-     Mark 9:22-24 NIV

The LORD is righteous in all his ways and loving toward all he has made.

The LORD is near to all who call on him, to all who call on him in truth.

He fulfills the desires of those who fear him; he hears their cry and saves them.

-     Psalm 145:17-19 NIV

God has made the first step. The next step is yours, my friend.

Jim Otis

Appendix A
Logical Answers, Solid Proofs:
Recommended Resources

There may be a number of issues that you wish to investigate further. As I mentioned, I fully believe that you can achieve a high level of intellectual satisfaction regarding the Christian faith and its claims. While I urge you not to use your questions merely as a smokescreen or as a mechanism to delay your choice, at the same time I encourage you in your healthy desire to know more about God. In the list that follows I think you will find references that speak to nearly any level of inquiry that you may desire to initiate.

Bell, James S. and Campbell, Stan. *No-Brainer's Guide to What Christians Believe.* Wheaton: Tyndale House Publishers, Inc., 2002.

Copan, Paul. *True for You, But Not for Me: Deflating the Slogans That Leave Christians Speechless.* Minneapolis: Bethany House Publishers, 1998.

Craig, William Lane. *Reasonable Faith: Christian Truth and Apologetics.* Wheaton: Crossway Books, 1994.

Craig, William Lane. *Hard Questions, Real Answers.* Wheaton: Crossway Books, 2003.

Craig, William Lane. *The Son Rises: The Historical Evidence for the Resurrection of Jesus.* Eugene: Wipf and Stock, 2000.

Kennedy, D. James. *Skeptics Answered: Handling Tough Questions About the Christian Faith.* Sisters: Multnomah Books, 1997.

Kumar, Steve. *Christianity for Skeptics: An Understandable Examination of Christian Belief.* Peabody: Hendrickson Publishers, Inc., 2000.

Lewis, C. S. *Mere Christianity.* New York: Collier Books, 1960.

Little, Paul E. *Know What You Believe: A Practical Discussion of the Fundamentals of the Christian Faith.* Colorado Springs: Cook Communications Ministries, 1999.

Little, Paul E. *Know Why You Believe.* Downers Grove: Intervarsity Press, 2000.

McDowell, Josh. *The New Evidence That Demands a Verdict.* Nashville: Thomas Nelson Publishers, 1999.

Southern, Randy. *The World's Easiest Guide to Understanding God.* Chicago: Northfield Publishing, 2003.

Strobel, Lee. *The Case for Christ: A Journalist's Personal Investigation of the Evidence for Jesus.* Grand Rapids: Zondervan, 1998.

Strobel, Lee. The Case for Faith: A Journalist Investigates the Toughest Objections to Christianity. Grand Rapids: Zondervan, 2000.

Appendix B
Clearing the Path: How the Bible Answers Difficulties, Excuses, Common Misconceptions and False Hopes

This Appendix is based on the concept of an old resource provided by R. A. Torrey for what used to be called "personal workers" or "soul winners." If Torrey's booklet wasn't the first tool of its kind, it was certainly one of the early versions. Since then many lists such as this have been compiled.

I have long wanted to update some of Torrey's references, and to add some meat to the bones. With that, I offer these Scriptural responses to a number of common problems and excuses that are made regarding the Christian life. Once again, though I'm tempted to embellish, I will leave the Scripture to speak for itself, with the exception of some reasonably brief questions or comments to help explain the context of an answer or to guide your thinking,

"For the word of God is living and active. Sharper than any double-edged sword, it penetrates even to dividing soul and spirit, joints and marrow; it judges the thoughts and attitudes of the heart. Nothing in all creation is hidden from God's sight. Everything is uncovered and laid bare before the eyes of him to whom we must give account."
-   Hebrews 4:12-13 NIV

Difficulties and Excuses

1.   I have committed too many sins for God to forgive me.   The things I've done simply are too evil for God to forgive.

1 Timothy 1:15-16 NIV

15 Here is a trustworthy saying that deserves full acceptance: Christ Jesus came into the world to save sinners-of whom I am the worst.

Romans 5:6-8 NIV

6 You see, at just the right time, when we were still powerless, Christ died for the ungodly. 7 Very rarely will anyone die for a righteous man, though for a good man someone might possibly dare to die. 8 But God demonstrates his own love for us in this: While we were still sinners, Christ died for us.

Isaiah 1:18 NIV

18 "Come now, let us reason together," says the LORD.   "Though your sins are like scarlet, they shall be as white as snow; though they are red as crimson, they shall be like wool.

John 3:16-18 NIV

16 "For God so loved the world that he gave his one and only Son, that whoever believes in him shall not perish but have eternal life. 17 For God did not send his Son into the world to condemn the world, but to save the world through him. 18 Whoever believes in him is not condemned, but whoever does not believe stands condemned already because he has not believed in the name of God's one and only Son.

Acts 10:43 NIV

43 All the prophets testify about him that everyone who believes in him receives forgiveness of sins through his name.

Luke 19:10 NIV

10 For the Son of Man came to seek and to save what was lost."

John 6:37 NIV

37 All that the Father gives me will come to me, and whoever comes to me I will never drive away.

Romans 3:22-26 NIV

22 This righteousness from God comes through faith in Jesus Christ to all who believe. There is no difference, 23 for all have sinned and fall short of the glory of God, 24 and are justified freely by his grace through the redemption that came by Christ Jesus. 25 God presented him as a sacrifice of atonement, through faith in his blood. He did this to demonstrate his justice, because in his forbearance he had left the sins committed beforehand unpunished- 26 he did it to demonstrate his justice at the present time, so as to be just and the one who justifies those who have faith in Jesus.

2. I don't feel anything. My heart must be too hard for me even to desire to come to Christ.

Ezekiel 36:26-29 NIV

26 I will give you a new heart and put a new spirit in you; I will remove from you your heart of stone and give you a heart of flesh. 27 And I will put my Spirit in you and move you to follow my decrees and be careful to keep my laws. 28 You will live in the land I gave your forefathers; you will be my people, and I will be your God. 29 I will save you from all your uncleanness.

Hosea 10:12 NIV

12 Sow for yourselves righteousness, reap the fruit of unfailing love, and break up your unplowed ground; for it is time to seek the LORD, until he comes and showers righteousness on you.

3. I'd like to come to Christ, but I have to clean up my act before I can do that. I'd be embarrassed to come to him with all of this sin in my life.

Ephesians 2:8-10 NIV

8 For it is by grace you have been saved, through faith-and this not from yourselves, it is the gift of God-9 not by works, so that no one can boast. 10 For we are God's workmanship, created in Christ Jesus to do good works, which God prepared in advance for us to do.

Matthew 9:12-13 NIV

12 On hearing this, Jesus said, "It is not the healthy who need a doctor, but the sick. 13 But go and learn what this means: 'I desire mercy, not sacrifice.' For I have not come to call the righteous, but sinners."

Luke 15:18-24 NIV

18 " 'I will set out and go back to my father and say to him: Father, I have sinned against heaven and against you. 19 I am no longer worthy to be called your son; make me like one of your hired men.' 20 So he got up and went to his father.

"But while he was still a long way off, his father saw him and was filled with compassion for him; he ran to his son, threw his arms around him and kissed him.

21 "The son said to him, 'Father, I have sinned against heaven and against you. I am no longer worthy to be called your son.'

22 "But the father said to his servants, 'Quick! Bring the best robe and put it on him. Put a ring on his finger and sandals on his feet. 23 Bring the fattened calf and kill it. Let's have a feast and celebrate. 24 For this son of mine was dead and is alive again; he was lost and is found.' So they began to celebrate.

Luke 18:10-14 NIV

10 "Two men went up to the temple to pray, one a Pharisee and the other a tax collector. 11 The Pharisee stood up and prayed about himself: 'God, I thank you that I am not like other men-robbers, evildoers, adulterers-or even like this tax collector. 12 I fast twice a week and give a tenth of all I get.'

13 "But the tax collector stood at a distance. He would not even look up to heaven, but beat his breast and said, 'God, have mercy on me, a sinner.'

14 "I tell you that this man, rather than the other, went home justified before God. For everyone who exalts himself will be humbled, and he who humbles himself will be exalted."

Isaiah 44:22 NIV
22 I have swept away your offenses like a cloud, your sins like the morning mist. Return to me, for I have redeemed you."

4. I'm not going to say I'm a Christian if I can't live up to the commitment. I'm not going to do this half way. I'm afraid I won't be able to do it.

John 10:27-29
27 My sheep listen to my voice; I know them, and they follow me. 28 I give them eternal life, and they shall never perish; no one can snatch them out of my hand. 29 My Father, who has given them to me, is greater than all; no one can snatch them out of my Father's hand.

Isaiah 41:10 NIV
10 So do not fear, for I am with you; do not be dismayed, for I am your God. I will strengthen you and help you; I will uphold you with my righteous right hand.

Isaiah 41:13 NIV
13 For I am the LORD, your God, who takes hold of your right hand and says to you, Do not fear; I will help you.

1 Peter 1:3-5 NIV

3 Praise be to the God and Father of our Lord Jesus Christ! In his great mercy he has given us new birth into a living hope through the resurrection of Jesus Christ from the dead, 4 and into an inheritance that can never perish, spoil or fade-kept in heaven for you, 5 who through faith are shielded by God's power until the coming of the salvation that is ready to be revealed in the last time.

2 Timothy 1:12 NIV

12 That is why I am suffering as I am. Yet I am not ashamed, because I know whom I have believed, and am convinced that he is able to guard what I have entrusted to him for that day.

Jude 24-25 NIV

24 To him who is able to keep you from falling and to present you before his glorious presence without fault and with great joy- 25 to the only God our Savior be glory, majesty, power and authority, through Jesus Christ our Lord, before all ages, now and forevermore! Amen.
NIV

2 Chronicles 32:7-8 NIV

7 "Be strong and courageous. Do not be afraid or discouraged because of the king of Assyria and the vast army with him, for there is a greater power with us than with him. 8 With him is only the arm of flesh, but with us is the LORD our God to help us and to fight our battles."

Romans 14:4 NIV

4 Who are you to judge someone else's servant? To his own master he stands or falls. And he will stand, for the Lord is able to make him stand.

2 Thessalonians 3:3 NIV

3 But the Lord is faithful, and he will strengthen and protect you from the evil one.

2 Thessalonians 3:5 NIV

5 May the Lord direct your hearts into God's love and Christ's perseverance.

1 Corinthians 10:13 NIV

13 No temptation has seized you except what is common to man. And God is faithful; he will not let you be tempted beyond what you can bear. But when you are tempted, he will also provide a way out so that you can stand up under it.

5. I can't do it. I'm just too weak to stick it out.

2 Corinthians 12:9-10 NIV

9 But he said to me, "My grace is sufficient for you, for my power is made perfect in weakness." Therefore I will boast all the more gladly about my weaknesses, so that Christ's power may rest on me. 10 That is why, for Christ's sake, I delight in weaknesses, in insults, in hardships, in persecutions, in difficulties. For when I am weak, then I am strong.

Philippians 4:13 NIV
13 I can do everything through him who gives me strength.

1 Corinthians 10:13 NIV
13 No temptation has seized you except what is common to man. And God is faithful; he will not let you be tempted beyond what you can bear. But when you are tempted, he will also provide a way out so that you can stand up under it.

6. I've tried before and I've failed. I couldn't make it.

Every believer has times of triumph and times of failure. A prolonged sense of failure and an inability to communicate with God is symptomatic of deeper issues. There is always the possibility that you may never have honestly surrendered your self-will to God's control. You may have been dishonest with God and with yourself. We are apt to doing that as human beings. Or, you may have come up against a roadblock in your progress and stopped the process of maturing, which grieves the Holy Spirit and hinders your relationship with God. Perhaps you fell away through neglect of God's Word, or through a disconnectedness with the Body of Christ or a lack of any structure to provide personal accountability.

Ephesians 4:30-32 NIV

30 And do not grieve the Holy Spirit of God, with whom you were sealed for the day of redemption. 31 Get rid of all bitterness, rage and anger, brawling and slander, along with every form of malice. 32 Be kind and compassionate to one another, forgiving each other, just as in Christ God forgave you.

Luke 22:31-32 NIV

31 "Simon, Simon, Satan has asked to sift you as wheat. 32 But I have prayed for you, Simon, that your faith may not fail.

Romans 8:3-4 NIV

3 For what the law was powerless to do in that it was weakened by the sinful nature, God did by sending his own Son in the likeness of sinful man to be a sin offering. And so he condemned sin in sinful man, 4 in order that the righteous requirements of the law might be fully met in us, who do not live according to the sinful nature but according to the Spirit.

Isaiah 40:29-31 NIV

29 He gives strength to the weary and increases the power of the weak. 30 Even youths grow tired and weary, and young men stumble and fall; 31 but those who hope in the LORD will renew their strength. They will soar on wings like eagles; they will run and not grow weary, they will walk and not be faint.

Psalm 119:11 NIV

11 I have hidden your word in my heart that I might not sin against you.

1 John 5:4-5 NIV

4 for everyone born of God overcomes the world. This is the victory that has overcome the world, even our faith. 5 Who is it that overcomes the world? Only he who believes that Jesus is the Son of God.

1 Peter 5:6-11 NIV

6 Humble yourselves, therefore, under God's mighty hand, that he may lift you up in due time. 7 Cast all your anxiety on him because he cares for you.

8 Be self-controlled and alert. Your enemy the devil prowls around like a roaring lion looking for someone to devour. 9 Resist him, standing firm in the faith, because you know that your brothers throughout the world are undergoing the same kind of sufferings.

10 And the God of all grace, who called you to his eternal glory in Christ, after you have suffered a little while, will himself restore you and make you strong, firm and steadfast. 11 To him be the power for ever and ever. Amen.

7. I just can't give up my lifestyle.

Galatians 6:7-9 NIV

7 Do not be deceived: God cannot be mocked. A man reaps what he sows. 8 The one who sows to please his sinful nature, from that nature will reap destruction; the one who sows to please the Spirit, from the Spirit will reap eternal life. 9 Let us not become weary in doing good, for at the proper time we will reap a harvest if we do not give up.

Philippians 4:13 NIV

13 I can do everything through him who gives me strength.

John 8:34-36 NIV

34 Jesus replied, "I tell you the truth, everyone who sins is a slave to sin. 35 Now a slave has no permanent place in the family, but a son belongs to it forever. 36 So if the Son sets you free, you will be free indeed."

1 Corinthians 15:1-2 NIV

15:1 Now, brothers, I want to remind you of the gospel I preached to you, which you received and on which you have taken your stand. 2 By this gospel you are saved, if you hold firmly to the word I preached to you. Otherwise, you have believed in vain.

Romans 1:16-17 NIV

16 I am not ashamed of the gospel, because it is the power of God for the salvation of everyone who believes: first for the Jew, then for the Gentile. 17 For in the gospel a righteousness from God is revealed, a righteousness that is by faith from first to last, just as it is written: "The righteous will live by faith."

John 16:33 NIV

33 "I have told you these things, so that in me you may have peace. In this world you will have trouble. But take heart! I have overcome the world."

Revelation 3:4-5 NIV

5 He who overcomes will, like them, be dressed in white. I will never blot out his name from the book of life, but will acknowledge his name before my Father and his angels.

8.   If I become a Christian I will be ridiculed. People will make fun of me, and may even discriminate against me. I could be persecuted.

Proverbs 29:25 NIV

25 Fear of man will prove to be a snare, but whoever trusts in the LORD is kept safe.

2 Timothy 3:10-17 NIV

10 You, however, know all about my teaching, my way of life, my purpose, faith, patience, love, endurance, 11 persecutions, sufferings-what kinds of things happened to me in Antioch, Iconium and Lystra, the persecutions I endured. Yet the Lord rescued me from all of them. 12 In fact, everyone who wants to live a godly life in Christ Jesus will be persecuted, 13 while evil men and impostors will go from bad to worse, deceiving and being deceived. 14 But as for you, continue in what you have learned and have become convinced of, because you know those from whom you learned it, 15 and how from infancy you have known the holy Scriptures, which are able to make you wise for salvation through faith in Christ Jesus. 16 All Scripture is God-breathed and is useful for teaching, rebuking, correcting and training in righteousness, 17 so that the man of God may be thoroughly equipped for every good work.

Matthew 5:10-16 NIV

10 Blessed are those who are persecuted because of righteousness, for theirs is the kingdom of heaven.

11 "Blessed are you when people insult you, persecute you and falsely say all kinds of evil against you because of me. 12 Rejoice and be glad, because great is your reward in heaven, for in the same way they persecuted the prophets who were before you.

13 "You are the salt of the earth. But if the salt loses its saltiness, how can it be made salty again? It is no longer good for anything, except to be thrown out and trampled by men.

14 "You are the light of the world. A city on a hill cannot be hidden. 15 Neither do people light a lamp and put it under a bowl. Instead they put it on its stand, and it gives light to everyone in the house. 16 In the same way, let your light shine before men, that they may see your good deeds and praise your Father in heaven."

Mark 8:35-38 NIV

35 "For whoever wants to save his life will lose it, but whoever loses his life for me and for the gospel will save it. 36 What good is it for a man to gain the whole world, yet forfeit his soul? 37 Or what can a man give in exchange for his soul? 38 If anyone is ashamed of me and my words in this adulterous and sinful generation, the Son of Man will be ashamed of him when he comes in his Father's glory with the holy angels."

Romans 8:18-31 NIV

18 I consider that our present sufferings are not worth comparing with the glory that will be revealed in us. 19 The creation waits in eager expectation for the sons of God to be revealed. 20 For the creation was subjected to frustration, not by its own choice, but by the will of the one who subjected it, in hope 21 that the creation itself will be liberated from its bondage to decay and brought into the glorious freedom of the children of God.

22 We know that the whole creation has been groaning as in the pains of childbirth right up to the present time. 23 Not only so, but we ourselves, who have the firstfruits of the Spirit, groan inwardly as we wait eagerly for our adoption as sons, the redemption of our bodies. 24 For in this hope we were saved. But hope that is seen is no hope at all. Who hopes for what he already has? 25 But if we hope for what we do not yet have, we wait for it patiently.

26 In the same way, the Spirit helps us in our weakness. We do not know what we ought to pray for, but the Spirit himself intercedes for us with groans that words cannot express. 27 And he who searches our hearts knows the mind of the Spirit, because the Spirit intercedes for the saints in accordance with God's will.

28 And we know that in all things God works for the good of those who love him, who have been called according to his purpose. 29 For those God foreknew he also predestined to be conformed to the likeness of his Son, that he might be the firstborn among many brothers. 30 And those he predestined, he also called; those he called, he also justified; those he justified, he also glorified.

31 What, then, shall we say in response to this? If God is for us, who can be against us?

Acts 14:22 NIV

22 strengthening the disciples and encouraging them to remain true to the faith. "We must go through many hardships to enter the kingdom of God," they said.

Acts 5:40-42 NIV

40 His speech persuaded them. They called the apostles in and had them flogged. Then they ordered them not to speak in the name of Jesus, and let them go.

41 The apostles left the Sanhedrin, rejoicing because they had been counted worthy of suffering disgrace for the Name. 42 Day after day, in the temple courts and from house to house, they never stopped teaching and proclaiming the good news that Jesus is the Christ.

2 Timothy 2:11-13 NIV

11 Here is a trustworthy saying: If we died with him, we will also live with him; 12 if we endure,

we will also reign with him. If we disown him,
he will also disown us; 13 if we are faithless,
he will remain faithful, for he cannot disown
himself.

Hebrews 12:2-4 NIV

2 Let us fix our eyes on Jesus, the author and
perfecter of our faith, who for the joy set before him
endured the cross, scorning its shame, and sat down
at the right hand of the throne of God. 3 Consider him
who endured such opposition from sinful men, so that
you will not grow weary and lose heart.

4 In your struggle against sin, you have not yet
resisted to the point of shedding your blood.

1 Peter 2:20-25 NIV

20 But how is it to your credit if you receive a
beating for doing wrong and endure it? But if you suffer
for doing good and you endure it, this is commendable
before God. 21 To this you were called, because Christ
suffered for you, leaving you an example, that you
should follow in his steps.

22 "He committed no sin, and no deceit was found
in his mouth."

23 When they hurled their insults at him, he did
not retaliate; when he suffered, he made no threats.
Instead, he entrusted himself to him who judges justly.
24 He himself bore our sins in his body on the tree, so
that we might die to sins and live for righteousness; by
his wounds you have been healed. 25 For you were like
sheep going astray, but now you have returned to the
Shepherd and Overseer of your souls.

9. If I become a born-again Christian it could hurt my business. People could question my stability and my judgment. It might hurt my chances of promotion, or even cost me my job.

Proverbs 29:25 NIV
25 Fear of man will prove to be a snare, but whoever trusts in the LORD is kept safe.

Mark 8:34-38 NIV
34 Then he called the crowd to him along with his disciples and said: "If anyone would come after me, he must deny himself and take up his cross and follow me. 35 For whoever wants to save his life will lose it, but whoever loses his life for me and for the gospel will save it. 36 What good is it for a man to gain the whole world, yet forfeit his soul? 37 Or what can a man give in exchange for his soul? 38 If anyone is ashamed of me and my words in this adulterous and sinful generation, the Son of Man will be ashamed of him when he comes in his Father's glory with the holy angels."

Matthew 6:28-34 NIV
28 "And why do you worry about clothes? See how the lilies of the field grow. They do not labor or spin. 29 Yet I tell you that not even Solomon in all his splendor was dressed like one of these. 30 If that is how God clothes the grass of the field, which is here today and tomorrow is thrown into the fire, will he not much more clothe you, O you of little faith? 31 So do not worry, saying, 'What shall we eat?' or 'What shall we drink?'

or 'What shall we wear?' 32 For the pagans run after all these things, and your heavenly Father knows that you need them. 33 But seek first his kingdom and his righteousness, and all these things will be given to you as well. 34 Therefore do not worry about tomorrow, for tomorrow will worry about itself. Each day has enough trouble of its own.

10. There is just too much to give up if I am to become a follower of Christ.

Mark 8:34-38 NIV

34 Then he called the crowd to him along with his disciples and said: "If anyone would come after me, he must deny himself and take up his cross and follow me. 35 For whoever wants to save his life will lose it, but whoever loses his life for me and for the gospel will save it. 36 What good is it for a man to gain the whole world, yet forfeit his soul? 37 Or what can a man give in exchange for his soul? 38 If anyone is ashamed of me and my words in this adulterous and sinful generation, the Son of Man will be ashamed of him when he comes in his Father's glory with the holy angels."

Psalm 84:11-12 NIV

11 For the LORD God is a sun and shield; the LORD bestows favor and honor; no good thing does he withhold from those whose walk is blameless.

12 O LORD Almighty, blessed is the man who trusts in you.

Romans 8:32 NIV

32 He who did not spare his own Son, but gave him up for us all-how will he not also, along with him, graciously give us all things?

1 John 2:15-17 NIV

15 Do not love the world or anything in the world. If anyone loves the world, the love of the Father is not in him. 16 For everything in the world-the cravings of sinful man, the lust of his eyes and the boasting of what he has and does-comes not from the Father but from the world. 17 The world and its desires pass away, but the man who does the will of God lives forever.

Hebrews 11:24-26 NIV

24 By faith Moses, when he had grown up, refused to be known as the son of Pharaoh's daughter. 25 He chose to be mistreated along with the people of God rather than to enjoy the pleasures of sin for a short time. 26 He regarded disgrace for the sake of Christ as of greater value than the treasures of Egypt, because he was looking ahead to his reward.

Philippians 3:7-14 NIV

7 But whatever was to my profit I now consider loss for the sake of Christ. 8 What is more, I consider everything a loss compared to the surpassing greatness of knowing Christ Jesus my Lord, for whose sake I have lost all things. I consider them rubbish, that I may gain Christ 9 and be found in him, not having a righteousness of my own that comes from the law, but that which is through faith in Christ-the righteousness that comes from God and is by faith. 10 I want to know Christ and the power of his resurrection and the fellowship of sharing in his sufferings, becoming like him in his death, 11 and so, somehow, to attain to the resurrection from the dead.

12 Not that I have already obtained all this, or have already been made perfect, but I press on to take hold of that for which Christ Jesus took hold of me. 13 Brothers, I do not consider myself yet to have taken hold of it. But one thing I do: Forgetting what is behind and straining toward what is ahead, 14 I press on toward the goal to win the prize for which God has called me heavenward in Christ Jesus.

Luke 12:16-21 NIV

16 And he told them this parable: "The ground of a certain rich man produced a good crop. 17 He thought to himself, 'What shall I do? I have no place to store my crops.'

18 "Then he said, 'This is what I'll do. I will tear down my barns and build bigger ones, and there I will store all my grain and my goods. 19 And I'll say to myself, "You have plenty of good things laid up for many years. Take life easy; eat, drink and be merry."
'

20 "But God said to him, 'You fool! This very night your life will be demanded from you. Then who will get what you have prepared for yourself?'

21 "This is how it will be with anyone who stores up things for himself but is not rich toward God."

11. The Christian life is just too hard.

Ephesians 2:8-10 NIV

8 For it is by grace you have been saved, through faith-and this not from yourselves, it is the gift of God-9 not by works, so that no one can boast. 10 For we are God's workmanship, created in Christ Jesus to do good works, which God prepared in advance for us to do.

Matthew 11:28-30 NIV

28 "Come to me, all you who are weary and burdened, and I will give you rest. 29 Take my yoke upon you and learn from me, for I am gentle and humble in heart, and you will find rest for your souls. 30 For my yoke is easy and my burden is light."

Proverbs 3:13-18 NIV

13 Blessed is the man who finds wisdom, the man who gains understanding, 14 for she is more profitable than silver and yields better returns than gold. 15 She is more precious than rubies; nothing you desire can compare with her. 16 Long life is in her right hand;

in her left hand are riches and honor. 17 Her ways are pleasant ways, and all her paths are peace. 18 She is a tree of life to those who embrace her; those who lay hold of her will be blessed.

Proverbs 13:15 NIV

15 Good understanding wins favor, but the way of the unfaithful is hard.

12. If I become a Christian, I will lose all my friends.

Not to sound too much like Mom, but, is that sort of friend worth having in the first place?

Proverbs 13:20 NIV
20 He who walks with the wise grows wise, but a companion of fools suffers harm.

Psalm 1:1-3 NIV
Blessed is the man who does not walk in the counsel of the wicked or stand in the way of sinners or sit in the seat of mockers. 2 But his delight is in the law of the LORD, and on his law he meditates day and night. 3 He is like a tree planted by streams of water, which yields its fruit in season and whose leaf does not wither. Whatever he does prospers.

1 John 1:3-4 NIV
3 We proclaim to you what we have seen and heard, so that you also may have fellowship with us. And our fellowship is with the Father and with his Son, Jesus Christ. 4 We write this to make our joy complete.

James 4:4-5 NIV
4 You adulterous people, don't you know that friendship with the world is hatred toward God? Anyone who chooses to be a friend of the world becomes an enemy of God. 5 Or do you think Scripture says without reason that the spirit he caused to live in us envies intensely?

13. This must not be for me. I just don't have any feeling.

This is a common misconception, molded into an excuse. The "feeling" aspect of the Christian faith is the product of one's commitment, thus, it follows rather than precedes your decision. The more meaningful sensibilities that the believer enjoys develop over time as the level of understanding and maturity in the Lord deepens. Notice in the following Scriptures the aspect of contingency (I've added some emphasis to help point it out): *As* we obey, follow and learn of him, our ability to feel and experience him grows, but the benefit always follows the act. In this respect, the ball is in *your* court!

Galatians 5:19-25 NIV

19 The acts of the sinful nature are obvious: sexual immorality, impurity and debauchery; 20 idolatry and witchcraft; hatred, discord, jealousy, fits of rage, selfish ambition, dissensions, factions 21 and envy; drunkenness, orgies, and the like. I warn you, as I did before, that those who live like this will not inherit the kingdom of God.

*22 But the fruit of the Spirit is love, joy, peace, patience, kindness, goodness, faithfulness, 23 gentleness and self-control. Against such things there is no law. 24 Those **who belong to Christ Jesus** have crucified the sinful nature with its passions and desires. 25 Since we live by the Spirit, let us keep in step with the Spirit.*

Acts 5:32 NIV

32 "We are witnesses of these things, and so is the Holy Spirit, whom God has given *to those who obey him.*"

1 Peter 1:8-9 NIV

*8 Though you have not seen him, you love him; and even though you do not see him now, **you believe in him and are filled** with an inexpressible and glorious joy, 9 for you are receiving the goal of your faith, the salvation of your souls.*

Ephesians 1:13-14 NIV

*13 And you also were included in Christ **when you heard the word of truth**, the gospel of your salvation. Having believed, you were marked in him with a seal, the promised Holy Spirit, 14 who is a deposit guaranteeing our inheritance until the redemption of those who are God's possession-to the praise of his glory.*

John 1:12-13 NIV

*12 Yet **to all who received him, to those who believed** in his name, he gave the right to become children of God- 13 children born not of natural descent, nor of human decision or a husband's will, but born of God.*

Acts 16:31 NIV

*31 They replied, "**Believe in the Lord Jesus**, and you will be saved-you and your household."*

14. I've really been seeking God, but I just can't find him.

God has been seeking humankind ever since the first sin in the Garden. God's first words to Adam and Eve after they sinned were "seeking" words. If you genuinely desire to find God, you will find him, so don't give up hope. You may want to examine your expectations. There is a lot of hype in certain media and in certain venues about how a relationship with God makes you feel, what it causes you to do, and what happens to you as a result of it. That is human showmanship, not a divine response, but if we don't know that our expectations can become confused.

Genesis 3:8-9 NIV
8 Then the man and his wife heard the sound of the LORD God as he was walking in the garden in the cool of the day, and they hid from the LORD God among the trees of the garden. 9 But the LORD God called to the man, "Where are you?"

Jeremiah 29:13-14 NIV
13 You will seek me and find me when you seek me with all your heart. 14 I will be found by you," declares the LORD, . . .
NIV

Luke 15:3-10 NIV
3 Then Jesus told them this parable: 4 "Suppose one of you has a hundred sheep and loses one of them.

Does he not leave the ninety-nine in the open country and go after the lost sheep until he finds it? 5 And when he finds it, he joyfully puts it on his shoulders 6 and goes home. Then he calls his friends and neighbors together and says, 'Rejoice with me; I have found my lost sheep.' 7 I tell you that in the same way there will be more rejoicing in heaven over one sinner who repents than over ninety-nine righteous persons who do not need to repent.

8 "Or suppose a woman has ten silver coins and loses one. Does she not light a lamp, sweep the house and search carefully until she finds it? 9 And when she finds it, she calls her friends and neighbors together and says, 'Rejoice with me; I have found my lost coin.' 10 In the same way, I tell you, there is rejoicing in the presence of the angels of God over one sinner who repents."

Luke 19:10 NIV
10 For the Son of Man came to seek and to save what was lost."

1 John 4:10 NIV
10 This is love: not that we loved God, but that he loved us and sent his Son as an atoning sacrifice for our sins.

Romans 5:6-11 NIV
6 You see, at just the right time, when we were still powerless, Christ died for the ungodly. 7 Very rarely will anyone die for a righteous man, though for a good man someone might possibly dare to die. 8 But God

demonstrates his own love for us in this: While we were still sinners, Christ died for us.

9 Since we have now been justified by his blood, how much more shall we be saved from God's wrath through him! 10 For if, when we were God's enemies, we were reconciled to him through the death of his Son, how much more, having been reconciled, shall we be saved through his life! 11 Not only is this so, but we also rejoice in God through our Lord Jesus Christ, through whom we have now received reconciliation.

15. I've missed my chance. I've rejected God too often, and now he has removed my opportunity to come to him. Even if I try, he won't receive me. I've "sinned away my day of grace."

John 6:37-40 NIV

37 "All that the Father gives me will come to me, and whoever comes to me I will never drive away. 38 For I have come down from heaven not to do my will but to do the will of him who sent me. 39 And this is the will of him who sent me, that I shall lose none of all that he has given me, but raise them up at the last day. 40 For my Father's will is that everyone who looks to the Son and believes in him shall have eternal life, and I will raise him up at the last day."

Romans 10:12-13 NIV

. . . – the same Lord is Lord of all and richly blesses all who call on him, 13 for, "Everyone who calls on the name of the Lord will be saved."

2 Chronicles 33:10-13 NIV

10 The LORD spoke to Manasseh and his people, but they paid no attention. 11 So the LORD brought against them the army commanders of the king of Assyria, who took Manasseh prisoner, put a hook in his nose, bound him with bronze shackles and took him to Babylon. 12 In his distress he sought the favor of the LORD his God and humbled himself greatly before the God of his fathers. 13 And when he prayed to him, the LORD was moved by his entreaty and listened to his plea; so he brought him back to Jerusalem and to his kingdom. Then Manasseh knew that the LORD is God.

16. I've really messed up. I'm convinced that I have committed the unpardonable sin. There is no hope for me.

The unpardonable sin is to commit unrepentant "blasphemy" against the Holy Spirit. Blasphemy, in this context, is to claim the attributes of God. In other words, it is to make yourself god, and to refuse both to recognize God for who he is and credit him for his work, *and* to persist in so doing even in spite of God's appeal to your heart as his Holy Spirit labors to reveal your error. It would be safe to say that if one is concerned about having committed the "unpardonable sin," one is not without hope. In general, this sin is unpardonable because it is not recognized, nor is there repentance.

Matthew 12:30-37 NIV

30 "He who is not with me is against me, and he who does not gather with me scatters. 31 And so I tell you, every sin and blasphemy will be forgiven men, but the blasphemy against the Spirit will not be forgiven. 32 Anyone who speaks a word against the Son of Man will be forgiven, but anyone who speaks against the Holy Spirit will not be forgiven, either in this age or in the age to come.

33 "Make a tree good and its fruit will be good, or make a tree bad and its fruit will be bad, for a tree is recognized by its fruit. 34 You brood of vipers, how can you who are evil say anything good? For out of the overflow of the heart the mouth speaks. 35 The good man brings good things out of the good stored up in him, and the evil man brings evil things out of the evil stored up in him. 36 But I tell you that men will have to give account on the day of judgment for every careless word they have spoken. 37 For by your words you will be acquitted, and by your words you will be condemned."

17. It's just too late for me.

Deuteronomy 4:29-31 NIV

29 But if from there you seek the LORD your God, you will find him if you look for him with all your heart and with all your soul. 30 When you are in distress and all these things have happened to you, then in later days you will return to the LORD your God and obey him. 31 For the LORD your God is a merciful God; he will not abandon or destroy you or forget the covenant

241

with your forefathers, which he confirmed to them by oath.

2 Peter 3:9 NIV

9 The Lord is not slow in keeping his promise, as some understand slowness. He is patient with you, not wanting anyone to perish, but everyone to come to repentance.

Revelation 22:17 NIV

17 The Spirit and the bride say, "Come!" And let him who hears say, "Come!" Whoever is thirsty, let him come; and whoever wishes, let him take the free gift of the water of life.

18.   I'd come to Christ, but when I look at Christians I see so many hypocrites. I can't stand the thought of it.

God will sort out the genuine from the counterfeit at the end of the age. In the meantime, he recognizes that there are hypocrites in the Church and tolerates them. God has cast a large net, which allows room for people to be exposed to the preaching and teaching of his Word and hopefully to experience a merciful and redemptive change of heart. God has also clearly indicated that your responsibility is for yourself and the state of your own heart and conduct. He will do the judging.

Matthew 7:21-23 NIV

21 "Not everyone who says to me, 'Lord, Lord,' will enter the kingdom of heaven, but only he who does the will of my Father who is in heaven. 22 Many will say to me on that day, 'Lord, Lord, did we not prophesy in your name, and in your name drive out demons and perform many miracles?' 23 Then I will tell them plainly, 'I never knew you. Away from me, you evildoers!'

Matthew 13:47-49 NIV

47 "Once again, the kingdom of heaven is like a net that was let down into the lake and caught all kinds of fish. 48 When it was full, the fishermen pulled it up on the shore. Then they sat down and collected the good fish in baskets, but threw the bad away. 49 This is how it will be at the end of the age. The angels will come and separate the wicked from the righteous."

Romans 14:10-13 NIV

10 You, then, why do you judge your brother? Or why do you look down on your brother? For we will all stand before God's judgment seat. 11 It is written:

"'As surely as I live,' says the Lord, 'every knee will bow before me; every tongue will confess to God.'"

12 So then, each of us will give an account of himself to God. 13 Therefore let us stop passing judgment on one another. Instead, make up your mind not to put any stumbling block or obstacle in your brother's way.

Romans 2:1-8 NIV

2:1 You, therefore, have no excuse, you who pass judgment on someone else, for at whatever point you judge the other, you are condemning yourself, because you who pass judgment do the same things. 2 Now we know that God's judgment against those who do such things is based on truth. 3 So when you, a mere man, pass judgment on them and yet do the same things, do you think you will escape God's judgment? 4 Or do you show contempt for the riches of his kindness, tolerance and patience, not realizing that God's kindness leads you toward repentance?

5 But because of your stubbornness and your unrepentant heart, you are storing up wrath against yourself for the day of God's wrath, when his righteous judgment will be revealed. 6 God "will give to each person according to what he has done." 7 To those who by persistence in doing good seek glory, honor and immortality, he will give eternal life. 8 But for those who are self-seeking and who reject the truth and follow evil, there will be wrath and anger.

Matthew 7:1-5 NIV

7:1 "Do not judge, or you too will be judged. 2 For in the same way you judge others, you will be judged, and with the measure you use, it will be measured to you.

3 "Why do you look at the speck of sawdust in your brother's eye and pay no attention to the plank in your own eye? 4 How can you say to your brother, 'Let me take the speck out of your eye,' when all the time there is a plank in your own eye? 5 You hypocrite, first take the plank out of your own eye, and then you will see clearly to remove the speck from your brother's eye.

19. God seems harsh, unjust and cruel to me. I'm not sure I want to submit myself to him.

Romans 9:20 NIV
20 But who are you, O man, to talk back to God?

Romans 11:33-36 NIV
33 Oh, the depth of the riches of the wisdom and knowledge of God! How unsearchable his judgments, and his paths beyond tracing out! 34 "Who has known the mind of the Lord? Or who has been his counselor?" 35 "Who has ever given to God, that God should repay him?" 36 For from him and through him and to him are all things. To him be the glory forever! Amen.

Isaiah 55:6-11 NIV
6 Seek the LORD while he may be found; call on him while he is near. 7 Let the wicked forsake his way
and the evil man his thoughts. Let him turn to the LORD, and he will have mercy on him, and to our God, for he will freely pardon.
8 "For my thoughts are not your thoughts, neither are your ways my ways," declares the LORD. 9 "As the heavens are higher than the earth, so are my ways higher than your ways and my thoughts than your thoughts. 10 As the rain and the snow come down from heaven, and do not return to it without watering the earth and making it bud and flourish, so that it yields

*seed for the sower and bread for the eater, 11 so is my
word that goes out from my mouth:*

*It will not return to me empty, but will accomplish
what I desire and achieve the purpose for which I sent
it."*

Job 40:1-14 NIV

40:1 The LORD said to Job:

*2 "Will the one who contends with the Almighty
correct him? Let him who accuses God answer him!"*

3 Then Job answered the LORD:

*4 "I am unworthy-how can I reply to you? I put
my hand over my mouth. 5 I spoke once, but I have no
answer- twice, but I will say no more."*

6 Then the LORD spoke to Job out of the storm:

*7 "Brace yourself like a man; I will question you,
and you shall answer me.*

*8 "Would you discredit my justice? Would you
condemn me to justify yourself? 9 Do you have an
arm like God's, and can your voice thunder like his?
10 Then adorn yourself with glory and splendor, and
clothe yourself in honor and majesty. 11 Unleash the
fury of your wrath, look at every proud man and bring
him low, 12 look at every proud man and humble him,
crush the wicked where they stand. 13 Bury them all
in the dust together; shroud their faces in the grave.
14 Then I myself will admit to you that your own right
hand can save you.*

Hebrews 12:5-15 NIV

*5 And you have forgotten that word of
encouragement that addresses you as sons:*

"My son, do not make light of the Lord's discipline, and do not lose heart when he rebukes you, 6 because the Lord disciplines those he loves, and he punishes everyone he accepts as a son."

7 Endure hardship as discipline; God is treating you as sons. For what son is not disciplined by his father? 8 If you are not disciplined (and everyone undergoes discipline), then you are illegitimate children and not true sons. 9 Moreover, we have all had human fathers who disciplined us and we respected them for it. How much more should we submit to the Father of our spirits and live! 10 Our fathers disciplined us for a little while as they thought best; but God disciplines us for our good, that we may share in his holiness. 11 No discipline seems pleasant at the time, but painful. Later on, however, it produces a harvest of righteousness and peace for those who have been trained by it.

12 Therefore, strengthen your feeble arms and weak knees. 13 "Make level paths for your feet," so that the lame may not be disabled, but rather healed.

14 Make every effort to live in peace with all men and to be holy; without holiness no one will see the Lord. 15 See to it that no one misses the grace of God and that no bitter root grows up to cause trouble and defile many.

20.   There are just so many things in the Bible that I cannot understand.   It makes it impossible for me to come to Christ when I don't understand what is supposed to be God's Word.

1 Corinthians 2:6-16 NIV

6 We do, however, speak a message of wisdom among the mature, but not the wisdom of this age or of the rulers of this age, who are coming to nothing. 7 No, we speak of God's secret wisdom, a wisdom that has been hidden and that God destined for our glory before time began. 8 None of the rulers of this age understood it, for if they had, they would not have crucified the Lord of glory. 9 However, as it is written:

"No eye has seen, no ear has heard, no mind has conceived what God has prepared for those who love him"- 10 but God has revealed it to us by his Spirit. The Spirit searches all things, even the deep things of God. 11 For who among men knows the thoughts of a man except the man's spirit within him? In the same way no one knows the thoughts of God except the Spirit of God.

12 We have not received the spirit of the world but the Spirit who is from God, that we may understand what God has freely given us. 13 This is what we speak, not in words taught us by human wisdom but in words taught by the Spirit, expressing spiritual truths in spiritual words. 14 The man without the Spirit does not accept the things that come from the Spirit of God, for they are foolishness to him, and he cannot understand them, because they are spiritually discerned. 15 The spiritual man makes judgments about all things, but he himself is not subject to any man's judgment: 16 "For who has known the mind of the Lord that he may instruct him?" But we have the mind of Christ.

Romans 11:33-34 NIV

33 Oh, the depth of the riches of the wisdom and knowledge of God! How unsearchable his judgments, and his paths beyond tracing out! 34 "Who has known the mind of the Lord? Or who has been his counselor?"

1 Corinthians 13:11-12 NIV

11 When I was a child, I talked like a child, I thought like a child, I reasoned like a child. When I became a man, I put childish ways behind me. 12 Now we see but a poor reflection as in a mirror; then we shall see face to face. Now I know in part; then I shall know fully, even as I am fully known.

Psalm 119:18 NIV

18 Open my eyes that I may see wonderful things in your law.

2 Peter 3:14-18 NIV

14 So then, dear friends, since you are looking forward to this, make every effort to be found spotless, blameless and at peace with him. 15 Bear in mind that our Lord's patience means salvation, just as our dear brother Paul also wrote you with the wisdom that God gave him. 16 He writes the same way in all his letters, speaking in them of these matters. His letters contain some things that are hard to understand, which ignorant and unstable people distort, as they do the other Scriptures, to their own destruction.

17 Therefore, dear friends, since you already know this, be on your guard so that you may not be carried away by the error of lawless men and fall from your secure position. 18 But grow in the grace and knowledge of our Lord and Savior Jesus Christ. To him be glory both now and forever! Amen.

Luke 11:9-10 NIV

9 "So I say to you: Ask and it will be given to you; seek and you will find; knock and the door will be opened to you. 10 For everyone who asks receives; he who seeks finds; and to him who knocks, the door will be opened.

Luke 24:30-32 NIV

30 When he was at the table with them, he took bread, gave thanks, broke it and began to give it to them. 31 Then their eyes were opened and they recognized him, and he disappeared from their sight. 32 They asked each other, "Were not our hearts burning within us while he talked with us on the road and opened the Scriptures to us?"

21. I have someone in my life who I can't forgive for the things they have done to me. If that's the price for my salvation, then I'll have to pass.

God takes an unforgiving spirit and attitude very seriously. It's necessary to understand that God is all about forgiveness. With God or without him in your life, an unforgiving spirit will destroy you spiritually and physically, so this is a serious problem, and should be given special attention if you're experiencing it.

Matthew 6:14-15 NIV

14 For if you forgive men when they sin against you, your heavenly Father will also forgive you. 15 But if you do not forgive men their sins, your Father will not forgive your sins.

Matthew 18:23-35 NIV

23 "Therefore, the kingdom of heaven is like a king who wanted to settle accounts with his servants. 24 As he began the settlement, a man who owed him ten thousand talents was brought to him. 25 Since he was not able to pay, the master ordered that he and his wife and his children and all that he had be sold to repay the debt.

26 "The servant fell on his knees before him. 'Be patient with me,' he begged, 'and I will pay back everything.' 27 The servant's master took pity on him, canceled the debt and let him go.

28 "But when that servant went out, he found one of his fellow servants who owed him a hundred denarii. He grabbed him and began to choke him. 'Pay back what you owe me!' he demanded.

29 "His fellow servant fell to his knees and begged him, 'Be patient with me, and I will pay you back.'

30 "But he refused. Instead, he went off and had the man thrown into prison until he could pay the debt. 31 When the other servants saw what had happened, they were greatly distressed and went and told their master everything that had happened.

32 "Then the master called the servant in. 'You wicked servant,' he said, 'I canceled all that debt of yours because you begged me to. 33 Shouldn't you have had mercy on your fellow servant just as I had on you?' 34 In anger his master turned him over to the jailers to be tortured, until he should pay back all he owed.

35 "This is how my heavenly Father will treat each of you unless you forgive your brother from your heart."

Ephesians 4:32-5:2 NIV

32 Be kind and compassionate to one another, forgiving each other, just as in Christ God forgave you.

5:1 Be imitators of God, therefore, as dearly loved children 2 and live a life of love, just as Christ loved us and gave himself up for us as a fragrant offering and sacrifice to God.

Philippians 4:13 NIV

13 I can do everything through him who gives me strength.

Common Misconceptions and False Hopes

1. I really think I can do this on my own. If I do right, if I manage to live a righteous life, God will certainly honor that and grant me salvation on the basis of my own righteousness.

Galatians 2:16 NIV

16 know that a man is not justified by observing the law, but by faith in Jesus Christ. So we, too, have put our faith in Christ Jesus that we may be justified by

faith in Christ and not by observing the law, because by observing the law no one will be justified.

Romans 3:19-20 NIV

19 Now we know that whatever the law says, it says to those who are under the law, so that every mouth may be silenced and the whole world held accountable to God. 20 Therefore no one will be declared righteous in his sight by observing the law; rather, through the law we become conscious of sin.

James 2:8-10 NIV

8 If you really keep the royal law found in Scripture, "Love your neighbor as yourself," you are doing right. 9 But if you show favoritism, you sin and are convicted by the law as lawbreakers. 10 For whoever keeps the whole law and yet stumbles at just one point is guilty of breaking all of it.

Matthew 22:37-40 NIV

37 Jesus replied: "'Love the Lord your God with all your heart and with all your soul and with all your mind.' 38 This is the first and greatest commandment. 39 And the second is like it: 'Love your neighbor as yourself.' 40 All the Law and the Prophets hang on these two commandments."

Matthew 5:20 NIV

20 For I tell you that unless your righteousness surpasses that of the Pharisees and the teachers of the law, you will certainly not enter the kingdom of heaven.

Luke 18:10-14 NIV

10 "Two men went up to the temple to pray, one a Pharisee and the other a tax collector. 11 The Pharisee stood up and prayed about himself: 'God, I thank you that I am not like other men-robbers, evildoers, adulterers-or even like this tax collector. 12 I fast twice a week and give a tenth of all I get.'

13 "But the tax collector stood at a distance. He would not even look up to heaven, but beat his breast and said, 'God, have mercy on me, a sinner.'

14 "I tell you that this man, rather than the other, went home justified before God. For everyone who exalts himself will be humbled, and he who humbles himself will be exalted."

Luke 16:15 NIV

15 He said to them, "You are the ones who justify yourselves in the eyes of men, but God knows your hearts. What is highly valued among men is detestable in God's sight.

1 Samuel 16:7 NIV

7 But the LORD said to Samuel, "Do not consider his appearance or his height, for I have rejected him. The LORD does not look at the things man looks at. Man looks at the outward appearance, but the LORD looks at the heart."

John 3:36 NIV

36 Whoever believes in the Son has eternal life, but whoever rejects the Son will not see life, for God's wrath remains on him."

Hebrews 10:28-29 NIV

28 Anyone who rejected the law of Moses died without mercy on the testimony of two or three witnesses. 29 How much more severely do you think a man deserves to be punished who has trampled the Son of God under foot, who has treated as an unholy thing the blood of the covenant that sanctified him, and who has insulted the Spirit of grace?

2. When everything is said and done, I just can't believe that God would damn anyone. I believe God is going to make sure that everyone is saved in the end.

Romans 2:4-11 NIV

4 Or do you show contempt for the riches of his kindness, tolerance and patience, not realizing that God's kindness leads you toward repentance?

5 But because of your stubbornness and your unrepentant heart, you are storing up wrath against yourself for the day of God's wrath, when his righteous judgment will be revealed. 6 God "will give to each person according to what he has done." 7 To those who by persistence in doing good seek glory, honor and immortality, he will give eternal life. 8 But for those who are self-seeking and who reject the truth and follow evil, there will be wrath and anger. 9 There will be trouble and distress for every human being who does evil: first for the Jew, then for the Gentile; 10 but glory, honor and peace for everyone who does good: first for the Jew, then for the Gentile. 11 For God does not show favoritism.

John 8:21, 23-24 NIV

21 Once more Jesus said to them, "I am going away, and you will look for me, and you will die in your sin. . . ."

23 "You are from below; I am from above. You are of this world; I am not of this world. 24 I told you that you would die in your sins; if you do not believe that I am [the one I claim to be], you will indeed die in your sins."

John 3:36 NIV

36 Whoever believes in the Son has eternal life, but whoever rejects the Son will not see life, for God's wrath remains on him."

John 5:39-40 NIV

39 You diligently study the Scriptures because you think that by them you possess eternal life. These are the Scriptures that testify about me, 40 yet you refuse to come to me to have life.

2 Peter 3:9-15 NIV

9 The Lord is not slow in keeping his promise, as some understand slowness. He is patient with you, not wanting anyone to perish, but everyone to come to repentance.

10 But the day of the Lord will come like a thief. The heavens will disappear with a roar; the elements will be destroyed by fire, and the earth and everything in it will be laid bare.

11 Since everything will be destroyed in this way, what kind of people ought you to be? You ought to live holy and godly lives 12 as you look forward to the day of God and speed its coming. That day will bring about the destruction of the heavens by fire, and the elements will melt in the heat. 13 But in keeping with his promise we are looking forward to a new heaven and a new earth, the home of righteousness.

14 So then, dear friends, since you are looking forward to this, make every effort to be found spotless, blameless and at peace with him. 15 Bear in mind that our Lord's patience means salvation, . . .

Ezekiel 33:11 NIV

11 Say to them, 'As surely as I live, declares the Sovereign LORD, I take no pleasure in the death of the wicked, but rather that they turn from their ways and live. Turn! Turn from your evil ways! Why will you die, O house of Israel?'

2 Peter 2:4-10 NIV

4 For if God did not spare angels when they sinned, but sent them to hell, putting them into gloomy dungeons to be held for judgment; 5 if he did not spare the ancient world when he brought the flood on its ungodly people, but protected Noah, a preacher of righteousness, and seven others; 6 if he condemned the cities of Sodom and Gomorrah by burning them

257

to ashes, and made them an example of what is going to happen to the ungodly; 7 and if he rescued Lot, a righteous man, who was distressed by the filthy lives of lawless men 8(for that righteous man, living among them day after day, was tormented in his righteous soul by the lawless deeds he saw and heard)- 9 if this is so, then the Lord knows how to rescue godly men from trials and to hold the unrighteous for the day of judgment, while continuing their punishment. 10 This is especially true of those who follow the corrupt desire of the sinful nature and despise authority.

Luke 13:3 NIV
   "But unless you repent, you too will all perish."

3. I'm trying really hard to be a Christian. I think I'm getting it. If God gives points for trying, I'm in!
   OR:
   I feel as if I'm doing OK. If God gives points for feelings, I'm in!
   OR:
   I'm doing the right things. I've recited the creed, I've joined the Church, and I'm hoping that will do it. If God gives points for joining up, I'm in!

Isaiah 12:2 NIV
   2 Surely God is my salvation; I will trust and not be afraid. The LORD, the LORD, is my strength and my song; he has become my salvation."

Proverbs 14:12 NIV

12 There is a way that seems right to a man, but in the end it leads to death.

Titus 1:16

16 They claim to know God, but by their actions they deny him. They are detestable, disobedient and unfit for doing anything good.

Acts 13:39 NIV

39 Through him everyone who believes is justified from everything you could not be justified from by the law of Moses.

1 John 5:11-13 NIV

11 And this is the testimony: God has given us eternal life, and this life is in his Son. 12 He who has the Son has life; he who does not have the Son of God does not have life.

13 I write these things to you who believe in the name of the Son of God so that you may know that you have eternal life.

4. I am a skeptic, but I'd like to know the truth. I wish I could find definitive answers about God and the Christian faith. I'd really like to know.

John 7:17 NIV

17 If anyone chooses to do God's will, he will find out whether my teaching comes from God or whether I speak on my own.

1 Corinthians 2:14 NIV

14 The man without the Spirit does not accept the things that come from the Spirit of God, for they are foolishness to him, and he cannot understand them, because they are spiritually discerned.

John 20:24-31 NIV

24 Now Thomas (called Didymus), one of the Twelve, was not with the disciples when Jesus came. 25 So the other disciples told him, "We have seen the Lord!"

But he said to them, "Unless I see the nail marks in his hands and put my finger where the nails were, and put my hand into his side, I will not believe it."

26 A week later his disciples were in the house again, and Thomas was with them. Though the doors were locked, Jesus came and stood among them and said, "Peace be with you!" 27 Then he said to Thomas, "Put your finger here; see my hands. Reach out your hand and put it into my side. Stop doubting and believe."

28 Thomas said to him, "My Lord and my God!"

29 Then Jesus told him, "Because you have seen me, you have believed; blessed are those who have not seen and yet have believed."

30 Jesus did many other miraculous signs in the presence of his disciples, which are not recorded in this book. 31 But these are written that you may believe that Jesus is the Christ, the Son of God, and that by believing you may have life in his name.

John 3:17-21 NIV

17 For God did not send his Son into the world to condemn the world, but to save the world through him. 18 Whoever believes in him is not condemned, but whoever does not believe stands condemned already because he has not believed in the name of God's one and only Son. 19 This is the verdict: Light has come into the world, but men loved darkness instead of light because their deeds were evil. 20 Everyone who does evil hates the light, and will not come into the light for fear that his deeds will be exposed. 21 But whoever lives by the truth comes into the light, so that it may be seen plainly that what he has done has been done through God."

John 5:43-44 NIV

43 I have come in my Father's name, and you do not accept me; but if someone else comes in his own name, you will accept him. 44 How can you believe if you accept praise from one another, yet make no effort to obtain the praise that comes from the only God?

Acts 26:9-20 NIV

9 "I too was convinced that I ought to do all that was possible to oppose the name of Jesus of Nazareth. 10 And that is just what I did in Jerusalem. On the authority of the chief priests I put many of the saints in prison, and when they were put to death, I cast my vote against them. 11 Many a time I went from one synagogue to another to have them punished, and I tried to force them to blaspheme. In my obsession against them, I even went to foreign cities to persecute them.

12 "On one of these journeys I was going to Damascus with the authority and commission of the chief priests. 13 About noon, O king, as I was on the road, I saw a light from heaven, brighter than the sun, blazing around me and my companions. 14 We all fell to the ground, and I heard a voice saying to me in Aramaic, '

Saul, Saul, why do you persecute me? It is hard for you to kick against the goads.'

15 "Then I asked, 'Who are you, Lord?'

" 'I am Jesus, whom you are persecuting,' the Lord replied. 16 'Now get up and stand on your feet. I have appeared to you to appoint you as a servant and as a witness of what you have seen of me and what I will show you. 17 I will rescue you from your own people and from the Gentiles. I am sending you to them 18 to open their eyes and turn them from darkness to light, and from the power of Satan to God, so that they may receive forgiveness of sins and a place among those who are sanctified by faith in me.'

19 "So then, King Agrippa, I was not disobedient to the vision from heaven. 20 First to those in Damascus, then to those in Jerusalem and in all Judea, and to the Gentiles also, I preached that they should repent and turn to God and prove their repentance by their deeds.

5. I don't believe this whole business, and I really don't care enough about it to spend a lot of time

researching it. God doesn't seem that important to me.

1 Corinthians 1:18-25 NIV

18 For the message of the cross is foolishness to those who are perishing, but to us who are being saved it is the power of God. 19 For it is written:

"I will destroy the wisdom of the wise; the intelligence of the intelligent I will frustrate."

20 Where is the wise man? Where is the scholar? Where is the philosopher of this age? Has not God made foolish the wisdom of the world? 21 For since in the wisdom of God the world through its wisdom did not know him, God was pleased through the foolishness of what was preached to save those who believe. 22 Jews demand miraculous signs and Greeks look for wisdom, 23 but we preach Christ crucified: a stumbling block to Jews and foolishness to Gentiles, 24 but to those whom God has called, both Jews and Greeks, Christ the power of God and the wisdom of God. 25 For the foolishness of God is wiser than man's wisdom, and the weakness of God is stronger than man's strength.

2 Corinthians 4:3-6 NIV

3 And even if our gospel is veiled, it is veiled to those who are perishing. 4 The god of this age has blinded the minds of unbelievers, so that they cannot see the light of the gospel of the glory of Christ, who is the image of God. 5 For we do not preach ourselves, but Jesus Christ as Lord, and ourselves as your servants for Jesus' sake. 6 For God, who said, "Let light shine out of darkness," made his light shine in our hearts to give us the light of the knowledge of the glory of God in the face of Christ.

John 8:21-24 NIV

21 Once more Jesus said to them, "I am going away, and you will look for me, and you will die in your sin. Where I go, you cannot come."

22 This made the Jews ask, "Will he kill himself? Is that why he says, 'Where I go, you cannot come'?"

23 But he continued, "You are from below; I am from above. You are of this world; I am not of this world. 24 I told you that you would die in your sins; if you do not believe that I am [the one I claim to be], you will indeed die in your sins."

2 Thessalonians 1:7-10 NIV

This will happen when the Lord Jesus is revealed from heaven in blazing fire with his powerful angels. 8 He will punish those who do not know God and do not obey the gospel of our Lord Jesus. 9 They will be punished with everlasting destruction and shut out from the presence of the Lord and from the majesty of his power 10 on the day he comes to be glorified in his holy people and to be marveled at among all those who have believed.

2 Thessalonians 2:9-12 NIV

9 The coming of the lawless one will be in accordance with the work of Satan displayed in all kinds of counterfeit miracles, signs and wonders, 10 and in every sort of evil that deceives those who are perishing. They perish because they refused to love the truth and so be saved. 11 For this reason God sends them a powerful delusion so that they will believe the lie 12 and so that all will be condemned who have not believed the truth but have delighted in wickedness.

Mark 16:16 NIV

16 Whoever believes and is baptized will be saved, but whoever does not believe will be condemned.

6. *I'm really not sure that God exists.*

Romans 1:18-22 NIV

18 The wrath of God is being revealed from heaven against all the godlessness and wickedness of men who suppress the truth by their wickedness, 19 since what may be known about God is plain to them, because God has made it plain to them. 20 For since the creation of the world God's invisible qualities-his eternal power and divine nature-have been clearly seen, being understood from what has been made, so that men are without excuse.

21 For although they knew God, they neither glorified him as God nor gave thanks to him, but their thinking became futile and their foolish hearts were darkened. 22 Although they claimed to be wise, they became fools

Psalm 19:1-4 NIV

The heavens declare the glory of God; the skies proclaim the work of his hands. 2 Day after day they pour forth speech; night after night they display knowledge. 3 There is no speech or language where their voice is not heard. 4 Their voice goes out into all the earth, their words to the ends of the world.

Psalm 14:1 NIV
The fool says in his heart, "There is no God."

7. I'm not sure whether God exists or not, but one thing I am sure of is that the Bible is just a book like any other book. It isn't the Word of God.

Mark 7:13 NIV
13 Thus you nullify the word of God by your tradition that you have handed down. And you do many things like that."

Matthew 24:35 NIV
35 Heaven and earth will pass away, but my words will never pass away.

1 Thessalonians 2:13 NIV
13 And we also thank God continually because, when you received the word of God, which you heard from us, you accepted it not as the word of men, but as it actually is, the word of God, which is at work in you who believe.

2 Peter 1:19-21 NIV
19 And we have the word of the prophets made more certain, and you will do well to pay attention to it, as to a light shining in a dark place, until the day dawns and the morning star rises in your hearts. 20 Above all, you must understand that no prophecy of Scripture

came about by the prophet's own interpretation. *21 For prophecy never had its origin in the will of man, but men spoke from God as they were carried along by the Holy Spirit.*

1 John 5:10 NIV
10 Anyone who believes in the Son of God has this testimony in his heart. Anyone who does not believe God has made him out to be a liar, because he has not believed the testimony God has given about his Son.

John 8:47 NIV
47 He who belongs to God hears what God says. The reason you do not hear is that you do not belong to God."

8. I think I'd rather just wait. I don't want to decide right now. I'll give it some time.

Isaiah 55:6-7 NIV
6 Seek the LORD while he may be found;
call on him while he is near. 7 Let the wicked forsake his way and the evil man his thoughts. Let him turn to the LORD, and he will have mercy on him, and to our God, for he will freely pardon.

Proverbs 27:1 NIV
Do not boast about tomorrow, for you do not know what a day may bring forth.

Proverbs 29:1 NIV

A man who remains stiff-necked after many rebukes will suddenly be destroyed — without remedy.

Matthew 24:36-44 NIV

36 "No one knows about that day or hour, not even the angels in heaven, nor the Son, but only the Father. 37 As it was in the days of Noah, so it will be at the coming of the Son of Man. 38 For in the days before the flood, people were eating and drinking, marrying and giving in marriage, up to the day Noah entered the ark; 39 and they knew nothing about what would happen until the flood came and took them all away. That is how it will be at the coming of the Son of Man. 40 Two men will be in the field; one will be taken and the other left. 41 Two women will be grinding with a hand mill; one will be taken and the other left.

42 "Therefore keep watch, because you do not know on what day your Lord will come. 43 But understand this: If the owner of the house had known at what time of night the thief was coming, he would have kept watch and would not have let his house be broken into. 44 So you also must be ready, because the Son of Man will come at an hour when you do not expect him.

Matthew 25:10-13 NIV

10 "But while they were on their way to buy the oil, the bridegroom arrived. The virgins who were ready went in with him to the wedding banquet. And the door was shut.

11 "Later the others also came. 'Sir! Sir!' they said. 'Open the door for us!'

12 "But he replied, 'I tell you the truth, I don't know you.'

13 "Therefore keep watch, because you do not know the day or the hour.

Luke 12:16-20 NIV

16 And he told them this parable: "The ground of a certain rich man produced a good crop. 17 He thought to himself, 'What shall I do? I have no place to store my crops.'

18 "Then he said, 'This is what I'll do. I will tear down my barns and build bigger ones, and there I will store all my grain and my goods. 19 And I'll say to myself, "You have plenty of good things laid up for many years. Take life easy; eat, drink and be merry."
'

20 "But God said to him, 'You fool! This very night your life will be demanded from you. Then who will get what you have prepared for yourself?'

1 Kings 18:21 NIV

21 Elijah went before the people and said, "How long will you waver between two opinions? If the LORD is God, follow him; but if Baal is God, follow him."

But the people said nothing.

James 4:13-14 NIV

13 Now listen, you who say, "Today or tomorrow we will go to this or that city, spend a year there, carry on business and make money." 14 Why, you do not even know what will happen tomorrow. What is your life? You are a mist that appears for a little while and then vanishes.

Luke 13:23-27 NIV

24 "Make every effort to enter through the narrow door, because many, I tell you, will try to enter and will not be able to. 25 Once the owner of the house gets up and closes the door, you will stand outside knocking and pleading, 'Sir, open the door for us.'

"But he will answer, 'I don't know you or where you come from.'

26 "Then you will say, 'We ate and drank with you, and you taught in our streets.'

27 "But he will reply, 'I don't know you or where you come from. Away from me, all you evildoers!'

John 12:35-36

35 Then Jesus told them, "You are going to have the light just a little while longer. Walk while you have the light, before darkness overtakes you. The man who walks in the dark does not know where he is going. 36 Put your trust in the light while you have it, so that you may become sons of light."

2 Corinthians 6:1-2 NIV

6:1 As God's fellow workers we urge you not to receive God's grace in vain. 2 For he says,

"In the time of my favor I heard you, and in the day of salvation I helped you."

I tell you, now is the time of God's favor, now is the day of salvation.

Hebrews 3:12-15 NIV

12 See to it, brothers, that none of you has a sinful, unbelieving heart that turns away from the living God. 13 But encourage one another daily, as long as it is called Today, so that none of you may be hardened by sin's deceitfulness. 14 We have come to share in Christ if we hold firmly till the end the confidence we had at first. 15 As has just been said:

"Today, if you hear his voice, do not harden your hearts as you did in the rebellion."

Ecclesiastes 12:1-5 NIV

*Remember your Creator
in the days of your youth,
before the days of trouble come
and the years approach when you will say,
"I find no pleasure in them"-
2 before the sun and the light
and the moon and the stars grow dark,
and the clouds return after the rain;
3 when the keepers of the house tremble,
and the strong men stoop,
when the grinders cease because they are few,
and those looking through the windows grow dim;
4 when the doors to the street are closed
and the sound of grinding fades;
when men rise up at the sound of birds,
but all their songs grow faint;
5 when men are afraid of heights
and of dangers in the streets;
when the almond tree blossoms*

and the grasshopper drags himself along
and desire no longer is stirred.
Then man goes to his eternal home
and mourners go about the streets.

Endnotes

Chapter One
[1] Acts 12:19-23

[2] Acts 25:13 through Acts 26:32.

[3] Based on: Asimakoupoulos, Greg, "Holding On," in Leadership Journal, Summer 1991.

[4] See Acts 20:7-12 for the story of Eutychus and the Apostle Paul.

Chapter Two
[5] Barnes, Albert, <u>Barnes Notes, Heritage Edition, Acts - Romans,</u> Edited by Robert Frew. (Baker Book House, Grand Rapids, 1983), page 289.

[6] Luke 19:10

Chapter Three
[7] Ephesians 3:20 NIV

Chapter Four
[8] Colossians 1:27 NIV

[9] Colossians 1:28-29 NIV

[10] The Great Evangelical Disaster, Francis Schaeffer, 1984, Crossway Books, Westchester, IL, page 150.

[11] *You've Got Mail.* dir. Nora Ephron, Warner Brothers presents a Lauren Shuler Donner production, a Nora Ephron film. Burbank, CA: Warner Home Video, c1999, video recording.

[12] Fitch, Janet, <u>White Oleander,</u> (Little Brown and Company: New York, 1999) pp. __ .

[13] Genesis 6:3 NIV

[14] 2 Corinthians 6:2 NIV

Chapter Five

[15] Yancy, Philip, <u>Rumors of Another World: What on Earth are we Missing?</u>, (Zondervan: Grand Rapids, 2003) pp. 41.

[16] Koon, Jeff; Powell, Andy, <u>Wearing of This Garment Does Not Enable You to Fly: 101 Real Dumb Warning Labels</u>, (Free Press: New York, 2003) pp. 81.

[17] Lewis, C. S., <u>Mere Christianity,</u> (HarperCollins: San Francisco, 2001 Edition) pp. 153.

[18] *Ephesians 2:8-9 NIV:* "For it is by grace you have been saved, through faith--and this not from yourselves, it is the gift of God--not by works, so that no one can boast."

[19] Lewis, pp. 154-155.

[20] Matthew 6:30; 8:26; 14:31; 16:8; 17:20; Luke 12: 28 KJV

[21] Mark 4:40 NIV

[22] Luke 7:20 NIV

[23] Luke 7:28a NIV

[24] Luke 7:32 NIV

[25] The word *zoe* in biblical Greek refers basically to the force of life in the soul and the spirit of man, or life of a spiritual rather than biological nature. It also has the idea of "highest and best" within it, representing all that Christ is as well as the sort of blessedness that Christ imparts through faith to those who become practicing believers.

[26] Lewis, pp. 162-163.

Chapter Six

[27] Hebrews 13:8 KJV

[28] 1 John 4:8 KJV

[29] Proverbs 23:18, Proverbs 24:14, Jeremiah 29:11

[30] Hebrews 4:15
[31] James 4:8 NIV
[32] John 17:3 NIV
[33] John 17:25-26 NIV
[34] Hebrews 4:15 NIV

Chapter Seven
[35] Matthew 16:13-18 NIV
[36] Matthew 13:47-50

Chapter Eight
[37] Judges 20:16 NIV
[38] *hamartia* in the Greek.

Chapter Nine
[39] Exodus 24:17 NIV
[40] Deuteronomy 4:24 NIV
[41] Hebrews 12:28-29 NIV
[42] Revelation 21:22-27 NIV
[43] Psalm 51:3-4 NIV
[44] Romans 6:23 NIV
[45] Romans 4:4 NIV

Chapter Ten
[46] Koon, pp. 83.
[47] John 8:34 NIV
[48] 2 Chronicles 33:1-20
[49] 2 Chronicles 33:11 NIV

Chapter Eleven
[50] These comments on Fourth Generation Warfare are paraphrased from the article *The Changing Face of War: Into the Fourth Generation*, by William S. Lind, Colonel Keith Nightengale (USA), Captain John F. Schmitt (USMC), Colonel Joseph W. Sutton (USA), and Lieutenant Colonel Gary I Wilson (USMCR), *Marine Corps Gazette*, October, 1989, Pages 22-26.

[51] Isaiah 5:18-21 NIV

[52] Romans 2:1 NIV

[53] Genesis 3:1-24

[54] Russell, Anna, *Psychiatric Folksong* quoted in Zacharias, Ravi, Can Man Live Without God (Word: Dallas, 1994), pp. 138.

Chapter Twelve

[55] *Toy Story*. dir. John Lasseter, Pixar Animation Studios, Burbank, CA: Walt Disney Home Video, c1995, video recording.

[56] Proverbs 21:2 KJV; Proverbs 20:2 KJV; Proverbs 14:12 and 16:25 KJV

[57] Psalm 36:1-2 NIV

[58]King, Carole, It's Too Late, lyrics from elyrics, http://www.elyrics.net/go/c/Carole%20King%20Lyrics/It's%20Too%20Late%Lyrics/

Chapter Thirteen

[59] Romans 7:23-24

[60] Adam Clarke's Commentary on Romans 7:24 (from Adam Clarke's Commentary, Electronic Database. Copyright (c) 1996 by Biblesoft)

[61] Ephesians 2:1-3 NIV

[62] See the history of the Philippian jailer in Acts 16:16-34.

Chapter Fourteen

[63] Matthew 10:34-36 NIV

[64] Exodus 20:4-6 NIV

[65] Ebert, Roger "The Passion Uncompromising," *Elkhart Truth*, Saturday, February 28, 2004, page D5

Chapter Fifteen

[66] 1 Corinthians 1:23 NIV

[67] Romans 9:32-33 NIV

[68] Isaiah 8:13-15 NIV
[69] 1 Peter 2:4-8 NIV
[70] Isaiah 53:1-12 NIV
[71] Hebrew-Greek Key Word Study Bible, Executive Editor Spiros Zodhiates, Th.D., AMG Publishers, Chattanooga, TN 37422, page 1875

Chapter Sixteen

[72] Associated Press article *Student honor rolls come under fire*, The Truth, Elkhart, Indiana, Sunday, January 25, 2004, page AA3
[73] Holwick's Sermon Illustrations, http://holwick.com
[74] http://msnbc.msn.com/id/4890829/
[75] 2 Corinthians 10:12 NIV

Chapter Seventeen

[76] This chapter based on Matthew 8:1-4. I am exercising liberty in proposing that the leper Jesus healed in this passage of Scripture may have been named Simon, and may be the same leper who later in his life entertained Jesus at his home in Bethany on the eve of the Triumphal Entry into Jerusalem.

Chapter Eighteen

[77] 1 Corinthians 10:14, 16 NIV
[78] John 3:16 NIV
[79] Kreeft, Peter, <u>Christianity for Modern Pagans</u>, (Ignatius Press: San Francisco, 1993) pp. 280-281.
[80] The juxtaposing of these four ideas comes from a sermon by Rick Warren that I once heard, although I cannot identify the source beyond that.

Chapter Nineteen

[81] Revelation 22:17 NIV
[82] This chapter is based on Matthew 26:6-16; Mark 14: 3-11; John 12:1-11. As I mentioned in Endnote 76,

I am taking license in surmising that this Simon the Leper and the leper Jesus healed in Matthew 8 are one and the same. It is a possibility, but not necessarily a probability.

About The Author

Jim Otis is Associate Pastor for Evangelism at Nappanee Missionary Church, and Senior Pastor of their CityChurch satellite congregation, both in Nappanee, Indiana. He holds B.A. and M.A. degrees in theology from Southwest Seminary. Jim has served as a church planter and is active as a city councilman. He and his wife, Pat, enjoy their grown children, their present and emerging grandchildren, ministry and missions, the Great Lakes, camping, and serving their community.

Jim facilitates ministry in several areas, including evangelism, apologetics, church planting, recovery and discipleship. He has a special interest in prayer and in trans-cultural community ministry. Together, he and Pat enjoy music ministry as well. Watch for his upcoming book, *PrayerCry* and developing website www.PrayerCry.com , including additional *Clear Path Home* evangelistic tools.

For further information on his ministries email jim@jimotis.com.

Jim Otis
1096 Bittersweet Circle
Nappanee, IN 46550
Phone 574-773-5343

Printed in the United States
31574LVS00001B/43-51

9 781418 480721